T H E · G R E A T
THEATRES
OF LONDON

THE · GREAT
THEATRES OF LONDON
AN ILLUSTRATED COMPANION

RONALD · BERGAN

FOREWORD
BY ANTHONY HOPKINS

Edited by
Robyn Karney

PRION

HALF-TITLE *Drury Lane: Theatre Royal in the 18th century*
TITLE PAGE *Wyndham's Theatre: stage curtain*
OPPOSITE *Whitehall Theatre: the auditorium*

EDITORIAL ACKNOWLEDGEMENTS
This book could not possibly have been achieved without the generous co-operation of theatre managers, photographers, archivists, press agents, researchers, and enthusiasts of the theatre, too numerous to mention. However, special mention must be made of the following people whose help went far beyond the call of duty

Nicky Frei at The National Theatre
Rosemary Squire of The Maybox Theatre Group
David Kinsey of the Stoll Group of Theatres
Brenda Thomas of the Stoll Group
Donald Cooper
Sue Hyman Associates
Yvonne Joyce of The Lyric Hammersmith
Kate Triscott of Michael Codron Ltd
Colin Mabberley and Jilian Edwardes-Jones of the Mander and Mitchenson Collection
Sarah Woodcock at The Theatre Museum
Peter Saunders Management
Clive Totman
Eric Auzins
Linda Doeser
Brian Rooney
Alex von Koettlitz
Tony Coghan
Naomi Buch
Michael Elwyn
Helen Bourne
Clive Hirschhorn
Janet Suzman
John Strange
Geoffrey Schneiderman
The wonderful electricians of the great London theatres without whom we could not have taken the photographs

This book was devised and produced by Multimedia Books Ltd.

Published in the United Kingdom 1990 by PRION, an imprint of Multimedia Books Limited, 32/34 Gordon House Road, London NW5 1LP

EDITOR Robyn Karney
DESIGNER Bob Burroughs
SPECIAL PHOTOGRAPHY Kirsty McLaren
PICTURE RESEARCH Pauline Simcock, Tessa Paul
PRODUCTION Zivia Desai

Text copyright © Ronald Bergan 1987
Compilation copyright © Multimedia Books Limited 198

British Library Cataloguing in Publication Data
Bergan, Ronald
    The great theatres of London.
    1. London, theatres, history
    I. Title
    792'.09421

ISBN 1-85375-057-3

Printed in Hong Kong by Imago

CONTENTS

FOREWORD

Architecture and Drama are brother arts, but like many siblings they don't always get along. The perfect performance, if there is such a thing, is the communion of actors, audience and the building itself. The acoustics, the sightlines, the comfort of the seats, the atmosphere of the auditorium, the service at the bars and the size of the dressing rooms all contribute to the success or failure of a production. Sometimes there is too great a contrast between the glamour and luxury of the front of house and the cramped squalor back stage. But, for an actor, there is nothing to equal playing before a laughing, weeping, snoring, coughing, shocked or enraptured audience in a space created for the purpose.

After years in the USA, I returned to find the architectural face of London changing rapidly, in some cases for the better. However, it is pleasing to see that the great London theatres, part of the glory of the city, remain virtually untouched by 'progress'. Fortunately, most of them are protected from the clutches of property developers. One doesn't have to believe in ghosts to feel a frisson when one enters these ornate and showy playhouses of yesteryear, the architectural equivalents

As Lambert Le Roux in Pravda *(1985)*

of how we imagine the flamboyant actor-managers like Tree and Irving to have been.

I have been lucky enough to have played at the Royal Court, which has a tradition going back to the era of Pinero and Shaw, combined with the reputation for radical contemporary drama; and for some years with Sir Laurence Olivier's National Theatre Company at the Old Vic, a theatre with one of the richest of histories. Now I've returned to a very different National Theatre on the South Bank, the concrete proof that modern theatres can have an ambience, excitement and personality of their own. That wonderful Olivier stage on which one can mount a vast battle or play the most intimate of scenes!

Yet we actors 'are the abstracts and brief chronicles of the time', and although Kean and Garrick and other great names that fill the pages of this book have come to dust, most of the theatres they played in still remain. The history of the theatre is also the history of theatres, a fact that this beautifully illustrated, entertaining and informative book celebrates.

Anthony Hopkins

With Judi Dench in Antony And Cleopatra *(1987)*

INTRODUCTION

A modern-day Wordsworth, standing upon Westminster Bridge, would still be able to contemplate 'ships, towers, domes, theatres and temples', although there are far more theatres than ever the poet dreamed of in 1807. In fact, London has more mainstream theatres than any other city in the world, most of them dating from the Victorian era, and clustered mainly in the West End – the area bounded by Oxford Street to the north, the Strand to the south, Regent Street to the west and Kingsway to the east – with Shaftesbury Avenue running like an arrow through this heart of the capital's playground.

Apart from the 40 or so theatres in the West End, there are the two great government-subsidised companies – the National on the South Bank and the Royal Shakespeare Company at the Barbican in the City – as well as the two famous opera houses, and important theatres at Blackfriars, Hammersmith, Sloane Square, Victoria, Hampstead and in the East End, plus the many fringe theatres that have mushroomed in and around London since the 1970s.

These many hives of theatrical activity are sustained by a standard of acting that has gained a justifiably high international reputation. In other words, theatre is alive and well and living in London, despite bitter economic realities and competition from cinema, TV, and video. Continuing queues at the box-office testify to the fact that there is no substitute for live entertainment.

The first playhouse, erected in London in April, 1576, was aptly called The Theatre. When it was pulled down in 1597, its timber was used to build the Globe, Shakespeare's famous Wooden O. The company there was led by Richard Burbage who was the first Hamlet, Lear and Othello, and one of the first in a long line of actor-managers who ran, and often owned, the theatres in which they performed. Laurence Olivier, in his tenure at the National Theatre at the Old Vic (which he quit in 1974), was probably the last of the species.

It took over a century for the playhouse to emerge from the unroofed, circular Globe into the familiar horse-shoe shaped auditorium with its tiered boxes. It was only in the 18th century that the theatre took on the trappings of pomp hitherto reserved for palaces and churches. In the 19th century, with the rise of the civic-proud middle classes, theatres were erected with

The Globe Theatre, original home of Shakespeare

Laurence Olivier and Vivien Leigh as Antony And Cleopatra *at the St. James' Theatre – alas, now demolished, in 1951*

porticos and columns echoing Imperial Rome, and decor of florid baroque motifs, a mode that continued until the end of World War I. There was a reaction in the 20s and 30s, when theatres went in for simpler lines and Art Deco interiors, while others were influenced by cinema architecture. The following generation broke away from the tyranny of the proscenium arch, moving towards the open stage and theatre in the round, as well as the more democratic seating of the raked auditorium. From the Theatre Royal, Drury Lane to the Barbican, London encompasses the visible history of theatre architecture.

In the process of researching this book, I would often have to visit theatres in the cold light of morning. Without the lights, the curtains or eager audiences, they resembled glamorous but ageing women caught before they are able to dress and make up. Thus it was possible to view the theatres as buildings of intrinsic interest, detached from their function, as one visits a cathedral when no service is in progress. However, an audience is an essential ingredient in making these architectural glories or extravagant follies come alive. 'The play's the thing', of course, but spectators are aware of the spatial relationship between the stage and the auditorium, the shape of the theatre and the decor, and the history, which makes theatregoing far more than what is happening over the footlights at a given moment.

I hope that my text, enriched immeasurably by the splendid photography taken especially for the book by Kirsty McLaren, will increase your pleasure in visiting the great theatres of London.

AUTHOR'S NOTE AND ACKNOWLEDGEMENTS

As a result of the cultural negligence practised by governments and property developers over the years, many valuable London theatres have been demolished. Happily, a fair number still remain. An act of Parliament passed in 1971 declared certain buildings to be a protected species in a two-tier grading system. Grade I means that the preservation of the building is a matter of public concern, and its permanent protection is thus ensured. Only three London theatres – Drury Lane, The Royal Opera House and the Haymarket – are designated Grade I. A listing in Grade II denotes a building to be of such architectural or historic importance that no rebuilding or demolition can be undertaken without sufficient reason. The only post-1920 theatres graded II in this book are the Savoy and the Phoenix. All those built prior to 1920 are listed Grade II.

The dates given in brackets after play titles refer to the opening of the particular production mentioned, and not to the first-ever production, e.g. *Hamlet* (1987).

Any work on the subject of the London theatres would be virtually impossible without the scholarly groundwork done by Raymond Mander and Joe Mitchenson. Their book, *The Theatres Of London* (New English Library), was my main source of information for which I am deeply indebted.

I am particularly grateful to the Stoll Moss Group, the Maybox Group, and the many managers and assistant managers who graciously showed me round their theatres, and allowed my photographer such liberty as well as the help of their electricians. My special thanks to George Hoare, who knows everything there is to know about London theatres in general, and Drury Lane in particular; and to my editor, Robyn Karney, who devised and controlled the project with perception and skill.

Ronald Bergan
London, 1987

THE ADELPHI

The king of musical comedy, George Edwardes, always maintained there was box-office magic in the word 'girl' and he was right – at least as far as the last 80 or so years of the Adelphi's history is concerned. Edwardes himself produced *The Quaker Girl* (1908), which ran here for 536 performances, followed by *The Girl In The Taxi* (1912) and *The Girl From Utah* (1913). The theatre's longest-running success was *Charlie Girl* starring Anna Neagle, which ran from December 1965 to early 1971, despite a lambasting from the critics. The 'Lambeth Walk Musical', *Me And My Girl* (1985), continued in the happy line of 'girl' hits.

The first theatre on the site in the Strand was built for a girl. John Scott, who made a fortune from the invention of a washing blue, built the Sans Pareil in 1806 for his stagestruck daughter. It opened with *Miss Scott's Entertainments* in which the talented Jane Scott sang songs, recited poems, spoke monologues written by herself, and danced. A series of melodramas

followed, with Miss Scott usually in the leading role.

In 1819, John Scott sold the theatre to two gentlemen called Jones and Rodwell, who gave it a facelift and renamed it the Adelphi. As the Lord Chamberlain's licence given to the theatre did not cover 'straight dramas', they were obliged to put on what were called burlettas, being plays containing no less than five pieces of vocal music in each act. This meant that even *Othello* had to be interrupted every few minutes by a song. This unhappy situation lasted until the monopoly of the Patent Theatres was broken in 1843. Despite this restriction, the Adelphi was one of the most popular theatres in London in the 1820s. William Moncrieff's *Tom And Jerry; Or, Life In London* (1821) ran a record 100 consecutive performances, but was surpassed a few years later by *The Pilot* (1825), adapted

The auditorium – an odd mixture of the garish and the restrained

from Fenimore Cooper's sea novel under the new management of Frederick Yates and Daniel Terry.

Adaptations from novels seemed to be the thing in the 1830s, with Charles Dickens' serials being the favourites. Moncrieff rapidly dramatised *The Pickwick Papers*, calling it *Sam Weller; Or, The Pickwickians* (1837), *Nicholas Nickleby* (1838) and *Oliver Twist* (1839). Dickens called Moncrieff 'the literary gentleman . . . who had dramatised 247 novels as fast as they had come out – some of them faster than they had come out.' In 1844, the famous French dancer Madame Céline Céleste, and the actor-manager Benjamin Webster, took over what a contemporary described as 'by far the most fashionably attended theatre in London',

'His (William Terriss) murder marked the
passing of the kind of melodrama so long
associated with the theatre where he died.'

Lynton Hudson, *The English Stage*

A typical Adelphi extravaganza around 1840

where they staged what came to be known as 'Adelphi
Dramas', mostly written by John Buckstone. Shaw
wrote that 'a really good Adelphi melodrama is of first-
rate literary importance because it only needs elabor-
ation to become a masterpiece.'

After Webster became sole manager, he decided to
demolish the theatre which had fallen into 'incurable
disrepair' and build a larger one in its place in 1858.
The New Adelphi was among the first London theatres
to evoke the epithet 'luxurious' from the press. During
the building's 42 years of existence it saw the successes
of Dion Boucicault's *The Colleen Bawn* (1860) and
The Octoroon (1861), the latter being the first play to
treat the American negro seriously. From 1879, the

handsome and debonair William Terriss, father of the
future actress Ellaline Terriss, appeared in a celebrated
series of melodramas. On 16 December 1897, life imi-
tated art when he was stabbed to death by a vengeful
actor as he was entering the stage door to appear in
Secret Service.

In 1901 the theatre was extensively altered and the
name changed to the Century, but public pressure
caused the old name to be restored. Under Otho Stuart,
whose 'management was distinguished for its judgement, enterprise and liberality', the Adelphi became
the home of Shakespeare and modern poetic dramas
from 1904 to 1908. Then musical comedy established
itself here, first under George Edwardes and later
Alfred Butt. As described above, 'girl' titles were popular, but *The Boy*, a musical version of Pinero's *The
Magistrate* (1917) ran 810 performances. Another 'boy'
was *Peter Pan* in the shape of Gladys Cooper at Christmas 1923. After two hit revues starring the husband-
and-wife team Jack Hulbert and Cicely Courtneidge,
and the musical *Mr Cinders* (1929), the theatre was
once again pulled down.

What arose in 1930 was a plain linear terra-cotta
structure designed by Ernest Schaufelberg. To detect
what the old facade looked like, one has only to glance
at the building next door, above an amusement arcade,
with its Corinthian columns and balustrade. Most of
the frontage of the Adelphi today is obscured by a large
sign, but the 1481-seat rectangular auditorium still
has attractive Art Deco fittings. The 1930s decor was a
perfect setting for its opening productions, many of
them modern musical comedies and revues produced
by Charles B. Cochran, including *Evergreen* (1930)
starring Jessie Matthews; Noel Coward's *Words And
Music* (1932) with Ivy St Helier, Doris Hare and 23-
year-old John Mills; *Follow The Sun* (1936) with Claire
Luce; and *Home And Beauty* (1937) in which Binnie
Hale sang the praises of 'A Nice Cup Of Tea'.

During the 1940s there was not much at the Adelphi
worthy of the theatrical history books other than Marie
Tempest's London farewell in a revival of Dodie Smith's
popular family comedy-drama *Dear Octopus* (1940);
Ivor Novello's *The Dancing Years* (1942), which ran for
most of the war; and Vivian Ellis' *Bless The Bride*
(1947). For most of the 1950s producer Jack Hylton
presented a series of variety shows featuring popular
radio and television personalities such as Jimmy

Jerome Kern's evergreen musical, Show Boat, *was revived in 1971. Cleo Laine (2nd right) starred as the half-caste Julie*

Edwards, Vera Lynn, Tony Hancock, Arthur Askey, Shirley Bassey, and the Tiller Girls, the English equivalent of the Radio City Rockettes.

Before musicals completely dominated the fare at the Adelphi into the 1980s, Bea Lillie as *Auntie Mame* (1958) held the stage here for two years. Van Johnson in *The Music Man* (1961) gave way to three home-grown musicals – *Blitz!* (1962), of which a critic commented that 'one comes out humming the sets by Sean Kenny', and *Maggie May* (1963), both by Lionel Bart, and the aforementioned *Charlie Girl*. Broadway returned with *Show Boat* (1971), *The King And I* (1973), and Stephen Sondheim's *A Little Night Music* (1975) starring Jean Simmons, Hermione Gingold, Maria Aitken and Liz Robertson. After Miss Robertson became Alan Jay Lerner's seventh wife, she played Eliza in her husband's *My Fair Lady* (1979). In 1982, the D'Oyly Carte Company made its valedictory appearances, ironically not at the Savoy across the road. The following year, Stephanie Lawrence had a personal triumph in the musical *Marilyn*, but, like its movie-star heroine, the show died prematurely, to be replaced by the long-running *Me And My Girl*.

Robert Lindsay and Emma Thompson in the smash-hit revival of Noel Gay's musical, Me And My Girl *(1983)*

THE ALBERY

Virtually back to back and boasting similar decorative late Victorian facades, are the Wyndham's Theatre, facing Charing Cross Road, and The Albery on St Martin's Lane. They have more in common than the same architect, W.G.R. Sprague. On entering the foyer of the Albery, one is faced by a bust of Sir Bronson Albery after whom the theatre was named in 1973. For its previous seventy years of existence, it was known as the New Theatre. The change of name was a fitting tribute to the dedicated theatrical dynasty that has played such a significant role in the history of the West End for more than a century.

The dramatist James Albery married sixteen-year-old Mary Moore in 1878. Seven years later, with three children and a husband whose health and income had been ruined by the demon drink, Mary joined actor-manager Charles Wyndham's company at the Criterion Theatre and soon became his leading lady and business partner. This successful collaboration enabled Wyndham to build the theatre that bears his name in 1899 and, four years later, the New on the vacant lot just behind it. After the deaths of James Albery (from cirrhosis of the liver) and Wyndham's first wife, Charles and Mary married in 1916. When his mother died, Bronson Albery (knighted in 1949) took control of the three theatres. His son Donald (knighted in 1977) followed in his footsteps and then Bronson's grandson Ian became managing director of what is called the Maybox Group, expanded to include the Piccadilly and Whitehall theatres.

Sprague, architect of eight extant London theatres, designed the New with a capacity of 877 seats, far larger than Charles Wyndham's other two theatres. It boasts a spacious entrance and a large and attractive dress-circle bar. Above the proscenium can be seen two golden angels, representing Peace and Music, with Cupids on either side. Much of the Louis XVI flavour of the white and gold decoration has been maintained, but the building lacks the intimacy, atmosphere and prettiness of its near neighbour. What it certainly does not lack is a rich heritage.

The newly-knighted Sir Charles Wyndham appeared opposite Mary Moore in the first production at the New in March 1903, a revival of a play called *Rosemary.* They were followed by such luminaries as Forbes Robertson, Mrs Patrick Campbell and Cyril Maude prior to Fred Terry (Ellen's younger brother) and his wife Julia Neil-

son taking over for six months annually from 1905 to 1913. Among their successes were *The Scarlet Pimpernel, Dorothy O' The Hall* and *Henry of Navarre,* in the latter of which Fred's daughter, Phyllis Neilson-Terry made her first appearance. Phyllis, a member of another legendary theatrical dynasty, was cousin to John Gielgud, who was to figure so prominently at the same theatre.

In 1915 Dion Boucicault, son of the playwright of the same name, became manager. His first presentation was a revival of *Peter Pan,* which flew high for a further four Christmas seasons, the Peter of 1917 being Fay Compton. Boucicault, known as 'Dot', also distinguished himself by producing a series of plays by leading playwrights such as Somerset Maugham (*Caroline* 1916; *The Land Of Promise,* 1917), A. A. Milne (*Belinda* 1918; *Mr Pim Passes By,* 1920), Sir Arthur Wing Pinero (*The Freaks,* 1918), and J. M.

A view of the prettily ornamented auditorium

'Here was a gathering together of 400 years of tradition, and the New seemed alive with distinguished ghosts.'

Bryan Forbes on the Old Vic tenancy

The great Sybil (later Dame Sybil) Thorndike gave well over 200 performances of her legendary St Joan *at this theatre in 1924*

Barrie (*The Old Lady Shows Her Medals*, 1917). The distinguished American actress Katharine Cornell made her only London appearance as Jo in *Little Women* (1919) and, in 1920, 21-year-old Noel Coward had a play of his produced in the West End for the first time. Despite a successful first night and good notices, *I'll Leave It To You,* with Coward himself in the lead, flickered out after five weeks. The failure was blamed on the economy-conscious Lady Wyndham (Mary Moore) who removed half the stage lighting. But she was also responsible for inviting Sybil Thorndike and her husband Lewis Casson to appear in Shelley's *The Cenci* (1922) and *Cymbeline* (1923) among other plays.

Fagin (Ron Moody) surrounded by his young apprentice pickpockets in Oliver! *Lionel Bart's musical ran for a record-breaking seven years*

Award-winning actor Anthony Sher in Torch Song Trilogy, *Harvey Fierstein's moving and funny play about a New York drag queen*

Then came Sybil's great triumph—her creation of the title role in Shaw's *Saint Joan* in March 1924, which ran for 244 performances.

Enter 21-year-old John Gielgud as Lewis Dodd (succeeding Noel Coward in the role) in Margaret Kennedy's *The Constant Nymph* (1925). His association with the theatre was resumed in the famous 'black and white' production of *Twelfth Night* (1932), followed by his first popular success as *Richard Of Bordeaux* (1933) by Gordon Daviot (a pseudonym for Josephine Tay.). The actor with the most mellifluent of voices then established himself as a star in *Hamlet* (1934), one of the longest runs ever of the play at 155 performances. After taking the title role in André Obey's *Noah* (1935), Gielgud invited Laurence Olivier to alternate with him as Romeo and Mercutio to Peggy Ashcroft's Juliet, with Edith Evans as the Nurse. The critics were less than kind to Olivier's Romeo, but it was during the run that he found his real-life Juliet in Vivien Leigh. Other notable pre-war Shakespeare productions here starred Edith Evans and Michael Redgrave in *As You Like It,* and Olivier and Judith Anderson in *Macbeth,* both in 1937.

When the Old Vic Theatre and Sadler's Wells were bombed out in 1941, the two companies sought refuge at the New, which became the site of many glittering evenings. For nine years, youthful queues gathering every morning at the side of the theatre was a common sight. They were rewarded with such memorable performances as Ralph Richardson's *Peer Gynt* (1944), Olivier and Richardson in *Uncle Vanya* (1946), and Edith Evans in *The Cherry Orchard* (1948). After the Old Vic returned to their renovated home, the high standard at the New was maintained. Female stars Katharine Hepburn in Shaw's *The Millionairess* (1952), Dorothy Tutin in *I Am A Camera* (1954) and Leslie Caron in *Gigi* (1956) sparkled brightly, before all gave way to the boy *Oliver!,* Lionel Bart's musical version of 'Oliver Twist', which ran from 1960 to 1967, breaking all records for this theatre.

In 1971, Olivier returned as head of the as yet homeless National Theatre company for a season which included his James Tyrone in Eugene O'Neill's *Long Day's Journey Into Night.* The next year, the RSC's production of Boucicault's *London Assurance*, with Donald Sinden and Judi Dench, transferred from the Aldwych and enjoyed a successful run, as did Somerset Maugham's *The Constant Wife* (1974) starring Ingrid Bergman. The theatre's change of name to the Albery did not alter its policy of presenting quality productions with top-ranking actors. In the 1980s, for example, were three sensitive American plays on serious issues: *Children Of A Lesser God* (1981), *Torch Song Trilogy* (1985) and *The Normal Heart* (1986).

THE ALDWYCH

There are few theatres in London that have two such distinct and diverse reputations as the Aldwych. For the pre-war generation it was the home of the 'Aldwych Farces'; for younger playgoers, the Aldwych is remembered as having been the London base of the Royal Shakespeare Company for 22 glorious years.

The Aldwych is the twin of the Strand Theatre on the opposite corner of the same block, not far from Drury Lane and the Royal Opera House. They were opened within seven months of each other in 1905, and designed by W. G. R. Sprague with identical facades and almost the same seating capacity of over 1000. The interior decoration of the Aldwych is a mixture of Georgian and French baroque, the dominant colour being a greyish blue with gilt ornamentation. A dual stairway ascends past three huge mirrors, and meets in the handsome plush Circle Bar under chandeliers from where one can look down into the vestibule from a cir-

cular ramp. The *Era* magazine in 1905 wrote that 'one of the innovations that will be greatly appreciated by the male members of the audience is a commodious smokers' gallery above the entrance hall.'

Today, on the walls of the Stalls Bar is a collection of paintings, playbills and photos of past successes lent by the Theatre Museum recently opened in Covent Garden. These range from a portrait of Ellaline Terriss in one of the Aldwych's first productions, *The Beauty Of Bath* (1906), through the famous Ben Travers farces and Alastair Sim in Bridie's *Mr Bolfry* (1943), to Vivien Leigh as Blanche du Bois in *A Streetcar Named Desire* (1949), and a pensive Alec Guinness in *Under The Sycamore Tree* (1952). There is little visible trace of the RSC's long and now historic sojourn here.

The gracious auditorium is an unusual and pleasing olive green

The Aldwych was built for actor-manager-dramatist Seymour Hicks in association with the famed American impresario Charles Frohman. Hicks and his wife, the beautiful Ellaline Terriss (born in the Falkland Islands in 1871), starred in the opening productions, often musical comedies such as *Blue Bell* (1905) and *The Gay Gordons* (1907). In 1909 Chekhov's *The Cherry Orchard* was given its first performance in England. Nigel Playfair, who was in the cast, related how the actors had little understanding of their roles, most of the audience walked out, and the critics complained that the play was gloomy and formless. It was to return to the Aldwych triumphantly in Michel Saint Denis' celebrated production for the RSC in 1961.

During the Great War the theatre put on a few popular revivals but was also used for a time as a club for

Looking down on the foyer, the elegant rotunda bar

'It was the happiest of choices for the RSC. A real theatre, not a culture bunker.'

Janet Suzman

John Barton's epic cycle of Greek dramas boasted an all-star cast, including Janet Suzman (illustrated) as Helen of Troy

Australian servicemen. In 1920, Sacha Guitry and Yvonne Printemps, the second of his four wives, came from Paris to appear in several of the Frenchman's pieces, including *Nono* (written when Guitry was 16.) However, with the transfer of *Tons Of Money* from the old Shaftesbury Theatre (destroyed by bombs in 1941), the Aldwych began its renowned reign as the home of English farce, a title it held until the Whitehall achieved a similar reputation in the 50s. In the main they were written by Ben Travers, and relied on mistaken identities, comical coincidences and ludicrous characters played by accomplished comedians such as Tom Walls, Ralph Lynn, Robertson Hare, Mary Brough and Winifred Shotter. *A Cuckoo In The Nest* (1925), *Rookery Nook* (1926), *Thark* (1927), *Plunder* (1928), *A*

Cup Of Kindness (1929) and others made the Aldwych one of the most popular places of entertainment in London until 1933.

There followed a lean period, despite the introduction of the Privilege Ticket – two seats for the price of one – until the wartime successes: Lillian Hellman's effective anti-Nazi play *Watch On The Rhine* (1942) starring Diana Wynyard and Anton Walbrook, and Lynn Fontanne and Alfred Lunt in Robert Sherwood's *There Shall Be No Night* (1943), written in response to the German invasion of Finland. This was followed by two fine actors in Shakespeare: Robert Donat in *Much Ado About Nothing* (1946) and Michael Redgrave as *Macbeth* (1947). America was represented strongly in the next few years. Gian Carlo Menotti introduced his opera double bill, *The Medium* and *The Telephone* in 1948, and there was the first English production of Tennessee Williams' steamy drama, *A Streetcar Named Desire* (1949), in which Vivien Leigh, in one of the few great female roles in English-speaking contemporary theatre, proved her powers as never before. Nineteen-fifty-five saw another American hit, *The Bad Seed,* by Maxwell Anderson but, in the same year, Christopher Fry's long-awaited *The Dark Is Light Enough,* despite Edith Evans' superb performance, was not a success.

Farce returned to the Aldwych in more ways than one in 1958 when Peter Sellers, appearing in the legitimate theatre (for the first and last time) in *Brouhaha,* stumbled onto the stage one night in a state of inebriation, and announced, 'I'm sloshed. Do you want my understudy to go on?' A vociferous 'No!', allowed him to give an outrageously funny performance, sometimes from the stalls!

For some years, the Shakespeare Memorial Theatre Company at Stratford-on-Avon had been looking for a second home in London. In 1960, when Peter Hall became artistic director, they acquired the Aldwych. Before moving in on 15 December, 1960 with Peggy Ashcroft as *The Duchess Of Malfi,* an apron stage (as at Stratford) was created by bringing the forestage forward to the line of the stage boxes, and eliminating the curtain. The interior was re-painted a dark olive, with the gilt left intact.

During their long tenancy, the Royal Shakespeare Company (so named in 1961) set new standards of Shakespeare production, and of other classical and modern plays, building up a brilliant ensemble

Roger Rees (foreground right) was Dickens' hero,
Nicholas Nickleby, *in the RSC's magnificent*
dramatisation of the novel

company of actors in the hands of inspired directors. Among the multitude of memorable productions were three directed by Peter Brook – a hippy *Midsummer Night's Dream,* a Samuel Beckett-like *King Lear* with Paul Scofield, and the revolutionary *Marat/Sade* which brought Glenda Jackson to the public attention. There was Pinter's *The Homecoming,* Brecht's *The Caucasian Chalk Circle,* the landmark sequence of eight of Shakespeare's history plays, *The Wars Of The Roses,* and their tenure culminated in their greatest hit, *Nicholas Nickleby* in 1979. The Aldwych also played host to Peter Daubeny's World Theatre season every summer from 1964 to 1973.

Since the departure of the RSC for the Barbican in 1982, the theatre has lost much of its glory, having housed a number of short-lived musicals and plays, but there are enough ghosts of the past within its walls to inspire another great era in its history.

After the departure of the RSC, Tom Courtenay at
the Aldwych gave life to the British comic-strip
favourite, Andy Capp. Val MacLane *was his 'missus'*

THE AMBASSADORS

King: What do you call the play?

Hamlet: 'The Mouse-trap.'

Little did Shakespeare know that Hamlet's sub-title for 'The Murder of Gonzago', would be the name of an Agatha Christie whodunnit which would occupy this dainty and diminutive theatre for over 21 years. From 25 November, 1952 to 25 March, 1974, until it moved a few yards across Tower Court to the St Martin's where it is still on(!), *The Mousetrap* and the Ambassadors were synonymous. Pity, in a way, that many plays and players did not have the opportunity to appear in one of London's most intimate and pretty playhouses during that marathon run.

The Ambassadors and the St Martin's were conceived by their architect, W. G. R. Sprague, as companions born at the same time in 1913, but World War I inter-

rupted the construction of the latter for three years. The Ambassadors is smaller and lower than its neighbour, both of them conveniently situated opposite the renowned Ivy Restaurant, favourite haunt of the theatrical elite. The theatre has an unfussy classical facade, crowned with a parapet and balustrade decorated with ball-shaped ornaments. Less restrained is the elegant Louis XVI auditorium, on the walls of which are festooned ambassadorial crests. For political reasons, these were painted out at the outbreak of war in 1914, and only reappeared in 1958. A beautiful chandelier shines down from the circular ceiling onto the 453 seats below. The horseshoe-shaped single balcony is reached by a few stairs up from ground level, while the stalls are actually underground.

Charles B. Cochran recognised that the charming

> ## 'In a little theatre like the Ambassadors, to have sitting together five or six people who don't laugh or applaud is demoralising.'
>
> C.B. Cochran

One of the tiniest foyers in London, looking onto the famous Ivy Restaurant

atmosphere and compact size of the Ambassadors would lend itself perfectly to 'intimate' revue when he took a lease on the theatre at the beginning of the war. Here, the great impresario introduced England to what was then a new genre of entertainment from Paris. *Odds And Ends*, starring French actress and singer Alice Delysia, was aimed at more sophisticated audiences than those attending the spectacular revues of the music halls. After 400 performances, it was followed by further Cochran 'miniature revues' called

The compact auditorium is decorated with exquisite attention to detail

A very young Richard Attenborough and his wife Sheila Sim, as Trotter and Mollie, in the original cast of The Mousetrap *(1952)*

More (Odds And Ends) and *Pell Mell*, also with Delysia, between 1915 and 1917. The French connection was continued in 1917 with the presentation of two translated plays, Anatole France's *The Man Who Married A Dumb Wife* and Eugene Brièux's *The Three Daughters Of Monsieur Dupont.*

Many productions of quality were staged during the regime of H. M. Harwood from 1919 to 1932, including his own plays. It was at the Ambassadors that West End audiences first applauded Ivor Novello (in *Deburau*, 1921), 24-year-old Hermione Gingold (in Lord Dunsany's *If*, 1921), Margaret Lockwood (*Family Affairs*, 1934), and 22-year-old Vivien Leigh (in Ashley Dukes' *The Mask Of Virtue*, 1935). Miss Leigh created a great impression, as did America's Paul Robeson in Eugene O'Neill's *The Emperor Jones* (1925). When Sydney Carroll took over as manager in 1932, he continued Harwood's good work by presenting revivals of *The Rivals*, *The Country Wife* (1934) and *The Soldier's Fortune* (1935). The last hit before World War II, was Margaret Rutherford in *Spring Meeting* (1938).

Hermione Gingold returned to the scene of her adult debut as a fully-fledged performer in the vastly successful *The Gate Revue* (1939), named after the little theatre in Villiers Street (bombed in 1941) from where

the show derived. The first revue, which had a young Michael Wilding in the small cast, was followed by *Swinging The Gate* (1940), *Sweet And Low* (1943), *Sweeter And Lower* (1944) and *Sweetest And Lowest* (1946), all with the inimitable Gingold. In 1949, she and Hermione Baddeley used the first major revival of Noel Coward's *Fallen Angels* as a joint showcase for their comic personalities.

Nobody ever imagined that a competent little thriller, adapted by Agatha Christie from her own short story *Three Blind Mice*, would enter the record books as the World's Longest Run. The small theatre, the able direction of Peter Cotes, the gripping old-fashioned murder yarn, and the snowball effect of a long run, helped *The Mousetrap* on its way to becoming a seemingly permanent tourist attraction. Richard Attenborough and his wife Sheila Sim were in the first of generations of casts. When the theatre was finally liberated from *The Mousetrap*, it took some years to catch the habit of success again. This came triumphantly with the transfer of the Royal Shakespeare Company's hit production of *Les Liaisons Dangereuses* (1986). This tale of French *libertinage* in the 18th century, adapted by Christopher Hampton and garlanded with awards, well and truly tied up the Ambassadors again.

Lindsay Duncan and Alan Rickman as the sexually decadent and scheming protagonists in Les Liaisons Dangereuses, *adapted from Laclos' intriguing novel*

THE APOLLO

The smallest of the six theatres that greet one on strolling up Shaftesbury Avenue from Piccadilly Circus, is the intimate Apollo with its French Renaissance facade. Four angels perched on two domed towers look down on 'London's Broadway' from the Apollo, which was opened in February 1901, a month after the death of Queen Victoria, thus making it the first playhouse of the new Edwardian age.

Henry Lowenfeld, the owner and manager, originally wished to call it The Mascot because of the badge of a clan of German gypsies, featuring a flying lizard supported by lions on a silver chain and buckle, that was incorporated into the decor to bring good luck. This can still be seen on the right hand side of the main entrance. The emblem's propitious properties did not

have much effect on the opening offering, *The Belle Of Bohemia,* a musical farce that flopped. Thereafter, the theatre has been lucky enough to have enjoyed a string of successes over the years.

Designed by Lewen Sharp, it is entirely without the pillars of its period that continue to obscure some seats in a number of older West End theatres. Another innovation was the orchestra pit, which Lowenfeld claimed to be 'a free adaptation of Wagner's construction of the orchestra at Bayreuth,' to provide a clearer, unmuffled sound from the instruments. It was hoped that, despite its 796-seat capacity which made it more suitable for straight plays, musical comedies would be the theatre's main attraction. George Edwardes, the manager who did more to popularize the genre than anyone else, pre-

The opulent but welcoming auditorium with (right) an example of the splendid interior statuary

sented *Kitty Grey,* which ran for 220 performances, and *The Girl From Kay's* (1902) that almost doubled the previous run. Further musical comedies and operettas followed, including André Messager's *Veronique* (1904) and Edward German's *Tom Jones* (1907), a long way from Fielding's novel, in which Cicely Courtneidge made her London debut.

From 1908 to 1912, Harry Gabriel Pélissier's *The Follies* were staged here, exceeding 500 performances a season. Pélissier, first husband of Fay Compton, who made her debut in his show, wrote most of the music, lyrics and satirical sketches as well as performing with his company, dressed mainly in Pierrot costumes against black and white curtains. It laid the foundations for intimate revue. After Pélissier died in 1913, aged 39, *The Follies* was disbanded. Mostly straight plays occupied the Apollo during the Great War, the most popular being the often-revived and twice filmed Harold Brighouse working-class Lancashire comedy, *Hobson's Choice* (1916), with Norman McKinnel as the patriarchal shoe shop owner.

Between the wars many theatrical treasures were dug out of a mixed bag. Ian Hay's thrice-filmed comedy, *Tilly Of Bloomsbury* (1919), continued for 400 performances, Phyllis Neilson Terry appeared in J. B. Fagan's *The Wheel* in 1922 and in a revival of *Trilby* in the same year, while Frederick Lonsdale's *The Fake* (1924) gave way to two revues in 1925. These were *By*

The Way starring Jack Hulbert and Cicely Courtneidge, and *Tricks* with 21-year-old dancer Marjorie Robertson (later Anna Neagle). The American 'borscht' circuit hit, *Abie's Irish Rose* (1927), Edgar Wallace's thriller *The Squeaker* (1928), Sean O'Casey's stylized World War I play *The Silver Tassie* (1929), Ivor Novello's *A Symphony In Two Flats* (1929) – not a musical – and John Van Druten's *There's Always Juliet* (1930) with Edna Best, Herbert Marshall and Cyril Raymond, provided the varied fare. In 1933 after Diana Wynyard, returning from Broadway, played Charlotte Brönte in Clemence Dane's *Wild Decembers,* Polish-born actress Elisabeth Bergner, forced to flee the Nazis, made her triumphant London debut in Margaret Kennedy's weepie, *Escape Me Never.*

Marion Lorne starred in a number of plays written for her by her husband Walter Hackett from 1934 to 1937, the best of which were *Hyde Park Corner* (1934), *Espionage* (1935) and *London After Dark* (1937). The last laugh at the theatre for some time came with Ian Hay's two-year run of *The Housemaster.* During the Munich crisis, Robert Sherwood's Pulitzer Prize-winner, *Idiot's Delight* (1938), with Raymond Massey, warned audiences of the coming of World War II, before they retreated into Patrick Hamilton's absorbing

*'One night during the run (of Home) at the
Apollo a man in the stalls suffered a heart
attack . . . The dream remained unbroken.
They continued with the play.'*

Garry O'Connor in *Ralph Richardson, An Actor's Life.*

*Two great Grand Old Men of the British theatre –
Sir Ralph Richardson (left) and Sir John Gielgud –
in David Storey's* Home

Victorian thriller *Gaslight* (1939).

The Apollo continued to shine dauntlessly through the dark years with *The Light Of Heart* (1940) by Emlyn Williams, *Old Acquaintance* (1941) by John Van Druten, and 670 performances of Terence Rattigan's *Flare Path* (1942). Nineteen-forty-four saw the first major revival of *Private Lives*, with John Clements and his wife Kay Hammond in the roles Noel Coward had written for himself and Gertrude Lawrence 14 years earlier; that year, too, the profitable theatre was taken over by Prince Littler. From the immediate postwar years to the present day, the theatre gained a reputation for being the home of long-running light comedies, the sort to attract 'the tired businessman'. These have included that lovable eccentric Margaret Rutherford as Miss Whitchurch in John Dighton's school farce, *The Happiest Days Of Your Life* (1948), Marie Lohr, Sybil Thorndike and Lewis Casson in *Treasure Hunt* (1949), and Hugh Hastings' service comedy *Seagulls Over Sorrento* (1950), which ran for over three years. Revue came back smartly with *For Amusement Only* (1956) featuring Ron Moody, and Peter Cook's *Pieces Of Eight* (1959) with Kenneth Williams and Fenella Fielding. The sequence of 'for amusement only' shows was broken briefly by Christopher Fry's

two adaptations from Jean Giraudoux, *Tiger At The Gates* (1955) with Michael Redgrave as Hector, and Vivien Leigh and Claire Bloom in *Duel Of Angels* (1958). In February 1962, Marc Camoletti's sex comedy *Boeing-Boeing* took the theatre over for a record-breaking 2035 performances before flying off to the Duchess in St Martin's Lane.

Although the theatre was redecorated in 1965, its repertoire has been little renovated. Apart from two visits by John Gielgud as the prudish headmaster in Alan Bennett's nostalgic satire *Forty Years On* (1968), and in David Storey's Pinteresque *Home* (1969) with his old friend Ralph Richardson; Eileen Heckart repeating her Broadway triumph in *Butterflies Are Free* (1970), and Albert Finney in *Orphans* (1986), the main fare has been bedroom farces with titles such as *The Mating Game* (1972), *Why Not Stay For Breakfast?* (1973), *Shut Your Eyes And Think Of England* (1977), and *Middle Age Spread* (1980) – proving that 'laughter is the English way of getting rid of something which makes them uncomfortable.'

Paul Scofield and Howard Rollins triumphed in
I'm Not Rappaport *(1986)*

THE APOLLO VICTORIA

Of all the theatres considered in these pages, the only one built specifically as a 'Picture Palace' is the Apollo Victoria, which opened as the New Victoria Cinema in 1930. By becoming an active theatre in 1981, it reversed a lengthy trend of theatres being transformed into movie houses – the Carlton, Dominion (since reclaimed), Leicester Square, London Pavilion, Prince Charles and Saville all went that way. But the Apollo eschewed its cinematic past with a vengeance when the auditorium was drastically reorganized to fit Andrew Lloyd Webber's hit musical on wheels, *Starlight Express* (1984). The multi-tiered set, ramps extending around the theatre, and the rock music, is a far cry from the golden age of cinema when the Mighty Wurlitzer rose up, its multicoloured lights flashing, before the 'big picture'.

The great decade of British cinema design was the 1930s, that of the USA the 1920s. It was said that the New Victoria was the most architecturally important cinema building to have been erected in Britain.

W. Lewis, the architect, provided a modern marble and concrete exterior and an auditorium, with a single long balcony, to seat 2,500 people. In those days full houses at weekends would usually cover costs for the whole week. The carefully wrought Art Deco designs and technically ambitious lighting effects created the impression of a sub-aquatic wonderland. It was decorated with fish, shell and sea flora motifs, and walls of marine colours. The circle, reached by a salmon pink staircase, had the design of an ocean liner with port holes on the doors. Despite some crass redecoration by the Rank Organisation in the 1950s, some of the original decor can be seen today. Above the Gents lavatory is a seductively reclining bronze mermaid in a Cleopatra hairdo, and in the foyer a nude female figure is in the process of throwing reels of film about.

When *Starlight Express* steamed in, 1000 seats were lost in order to accommodate the roller-skating ramps

The elaborate art deco stairway to the auditorium

29

'People do not want this sort of thing: they want architecture with marble columns, gilt and mirrors. This won't pay.'

Sidney Bernstein to the architect

that spill into the auditorium. Races take place along these ramps and over a railway bridge, while large video screens allow the audience to watch their progress. Small model trains also move along tracks around the theatre. New lighting had to be installed and the overhang of the circle painted black. According to the press handout: 'The scenic artists used over 750 gallons of paint and varnish to complement the brilliant lighting effects. The giant skating "bowl" . . . is built with the precision of an ocean-going yacht, with some 2,100 sheets (over 2½ acres) of board being used in its construction . . . The components of the huge set have to lift, tilt and revolve – and be safe. The central track handrail alone has to move up and down 70 times each week!' No more are musicals satisfied with a boy, a girl, a park bench and a chorus. However, for a show that uses every new theatrical device at its disposal (like *Time* at the Dominion, and *Chess* at the Prince Edward – also former cinemas) it extols the age of the steam

A pair of roller-skaters negotiate a section of the elaborate track in Starlight Express

Sholom Aleichem's immortal Jewish milkman, Tevye, was given life by Topol (foreground in red cap) in the 1983 revival of Fiddler On The Roof

Aloft the gentlemen's toilets, a bronze 'Egyptian' mermaid guards the entrance

train, rather like a wide-screen spectacular movie with Dolby sound praising the merits of steam radio.

It could be said that *Starlight Express* has put the Apollo Victoria 'on the map'. Before that, the super-cinema, built at a cost of a quarter-of-a-million pounds, opposite Victoria Station, had a less than glorious past. As a cinema, after the honeymoon cruise was over, it struggled for many years, interrupted occasionally by the London Festival Ballet, pop concerts and cabarets. Its location and size found it failing to compete with first, television, then the smaller cinemas and the video boom. The New Victoria closed down in 1976, emerging five years later, under its new name when bought by Apollo Leisure (UK) Ltd.

It opened with a Shirley Bassey recital, followed by the revival of Rodgers and Hammerstein's *The Sound Of Music* (1981) with Petula Clark as the singing novice. Another failed attempt to resurrect a hit musical was *Camelot* (1982) starring Richard Harris. Diminutive dancer Wayne Sleep showed his range in *Dash*, and the Israeli star, Topol returned to play Tevye for the second time in London in a short but successful season of *Fiddler On The Roof* (both 1983), before the Apollo was filled with – in the words of Lloyd Webber and Richard Stilgoe's song – 'A Lotta Locomotion'.

THE BARBICAN

After emerging from the Barbican underground station, follow the yellow brick line, alongside towering apartment buildings, and you will suddenly come across an artificial lake, fountains, and the wonder of a modern arts complex complete with concert hall, art galleries, libraries, cinemas, restaurants, conference halls and theatres. Until the new Barbican Centre's automatic doors slid open to the public in March 1982, the City, the commercial heart of London that throbs with capitalist activity by day, was a cultural desert by night. Adolph Hitler was indirectly responsible for the creation of this artistic oasis.

Before World War II, Cripplegate, situated north of St Paul's Cathedral and the Bank of England, was a busy area of small streets and warehouses – the home of the rag trade – in the centre of which stood St Giles' Church. In December 1940, the district was bombed unmercifully by the Luftwaffe, an attack that flattened most of the buildings, but spared St Giles. It still stands

demurely behind the modern centre. The surroundings lay as a neglected bomb site for 12 years before various proposals were put forward for development. Office blocks seemed the inevitable fate of the once lively area until, in 1959, Duncan Sandys, the Minister for Housing and Local Development, suggested that 'a genuine residential neighbourhood, incorporating schools, shops, open spaces and other amenities' should be created 'even if this means foregoing a more remunerative return on the land.'

In April 1959, the Corporation of the City of London approved a scheme proposed by architects Chamberlin, Powell and Bon for apartment blocks and an arts centre, including a concert hall and theatre as the new premises for the Guildhall School of Music and Drama. Three years later it was decided that the Guildhall School 'be planned as a self-contained entity which would not share the use of the theatre or concert hall, so that these two elements would be available for full-

The London Symphony Orchestra plays in the Concert Hall

time occupation by professional companies.' In 1964 the Royal Shakespeare Company and the London Symphony Orchestra, then sharing the Royal Festival Hall with other orchestras, became involved in the planning of the theatre and concert hall. It was a rare opportunity for the future occupants to actually play a part in the design of their new homes.

Of the two large subsidized theatres, the National company was installed at the Old Vic while waiting for its new building; the RSC was doing its best to function in its rather cramped London quarters at the Aldwych. Peter Hall, then the artistic director, and the stage designer John Bury, worked in close contact with the architects. Out of their discussions came the basic fan-shape or 'modified horseshoe' and, as theatre architect Victor Glasstone wrote, 'most dramatically, the entirely novel scheme of shallow balconies, each thrusting forward one over the other; a concept quite unique, as far as I know.' However, it would take 18 years after its inception before the RSC could move in.

There were many construction difficulties to surmount along the way to completion of this vast and daring concept that eventually became the Barbican Centre. The name derives from the location in proxim-

ity to where Roman walls once existed on which were built *barbicans* or watch towers. Foundations had to be sunk up to 80 feet below ground level without disturbing the foundations of the nearby buildings. Literally crowning it all, is the widest, unsupported flat roof in Europe.

The auditorium of the main theatre, with a total seating capacity of 1166, consists of raked stalls, and three narrow circles of only two rows each jutting forward one above the other towards the stage – the most distant seat being a mere 65 feet away. There is no permanent orchestra pit, but the first three rows of the stalls can be removed to provide one, and there is provision for a proscenium arch. The interior finish was arrived at after consultation with Trevor Nunn, who became artistic director of the RSC in 1968. He asked that the house lighting 'glitter not dazzle', and for the walls to be darker than the pale yew originally chosen. They were replaced by a sensuous Peruvian walnut. There are no aisles in the stalls and each row leads to its own individual door, held open before the performance and during the intervals by an electromagnet. When the houselights dim, all the doors close in unison caused by the desensitizing of the magnets. This creates a theatrical atmosphere even before the stage is lit. As in most modern theatres there is no curtain, but at intervals a huge black stainless steel fire curtain rises

> *'The absence of aisles in the stalls will obviate
> the horror of actors fooling about in them –
> a dated practice . . . that should be forbidden.'*
>
> Victor Glasstone

A performance in progress in the RSC auditorium

from the floor to meet another descending from the ceiling.

In fact, the whole building is a show in itself. One is constantly surprised when wandering around its spacious and comfortable halls. In the main foyer is an immense metal and acrylic Sculpture For Lighting by Michel J. Santry suspended from the ceiling, and there are often art exhibitions to be seen or musicians to be heard in odd corners. Also worth seeing and 'hearing' is the magnificent wood-panelled 2026-seat concert hall. On a summer's day, one can sit on the Lakeside Terrace, wander in the beautiful glass conservatory, or enjoy a meal in the Cut Above restaurant with its panoramic views of St Paul's and St Giles' Church. All of which gives the lie to those oft-heard derogatory cries of 'airport architecture', although it does have the feel of an 'Arts Hilton'.

But the play's the thing! As befits the Royal Shakespeare Company's name, the Bard is continuously in the repertoire, always looked at from a fresh vantage point that justifies critic Jan Kott's calling him 'the greatest living playwright.' From the opening productions of both parts of *Henry IV* in 1982 to the delightful *Merry Wives Of Windsor* (1986-1987) set in 1959, the Britain of the new Elizabethans, dust has never been allowed to settle on Shakespeare's works. Other memorable evenings which have thrust London's youngest

The foyer at the Barbican Centre, showing the specially commissioned light sculpture

Anthony Sher gave a compelling portrayal of Richard III for the RSC in 1985

adaptation of Laclos' *Les Liaisons Dangereuses* (1986). The latter was originally given at The Pit, the RSC's intimate (200 seats) and flexible studio theatre situated under the main auditorium.

The two last-named productions have helped greatly to fill the coffers of the RSC, which relies on subsidies from the Arts Council for about 40% of its annual costs. Box-office takings alone, although healthy, cannot meet the the expenses of the ambitious projects and repertory system. In 1987, the Company had a total of 47 productions playing in Great Britain and overseas. Situated in this magnificent ultra-modern theatre at the Barbican, the RSC has come a long way since a group of players was selected to play the works of Shakespeare in an ugly Victorian Gothic building in Stratford-on-Avon 108 years ago.

Mistress Quickly (Sheila Steafel) and Falstaff (Peter Jeffrey) in the RSC's modern-dress production of The Merry Wives of Windsor *(1986)*

theatre into instant theatrical fame were an Edwardian *All's Well That Ends Well* (1982) with Peggy Ashcroft as the Countess, a circus *Comedy Of Errors* (1984), the extraordinarily dextrous crutch-wielding Anthony Sher as *Richard III* (1984-1985), and Jeremy Irons' poignant *Richard II* (1987). Apart from Shakespeare, Judi Dench triumphed as Brecht's *Mother Courage,* and Derek Jacobi shone as *Cyrano de Bergerac,* both marathon performances in 1984, and there was an adventurous Jean Genet retrospective in 1987.

Of course, it hasn't been bouquets all the way. There was the unhappy first night of *The Happiest Days Of Your Life,* when the juvenile lead forgot most of his lines. He turned to the audience at one stage and said, 'You've heard of the actor's nightmare. Well, I'm living it.' The critics also got their teeth into Peter Barnes' desperately unfunny version of short Feydeau farces entitled *Scenes From A Marriage* (1985). There was criticism when Trevor Nunn and John Caird directed the English version of the French musical *Les Miserables* by Alain Boublil and Claude Michel Shonberg – some commentators considering it an inappropriately commercial venture. It turned out to be one of the company's greatest successes, transferring for a long run at London's Palace Theatre and on Broadway. Another hit that started small and moved to the West End and Broadway was Christopher Hampton's skilful

THE CAMBRIDGE

On a corner, where seven streets meet to form what is known as Seven Dials, stands the newly-restored Cambridge Theatre, which has been at the crossroads many times in its 57-year existence. It was the second of six theatres built in London in 1930, each claiming to be more modern than the next. The others were the Prince Edward, the Phoenix, the Whitehall, the Adelphi, and the Leicester Square (now a cinema). The claim to modernity of the Cambridge (designed by the firm of Wimperis, Simpson and Guthrie) was its use of concrete and steel, its clean lines, lively gold and silver decor by Serge Chermayeff (much of it painted over in red in 1950), and its concealed lighting (replaced by gilt candelabras and chandeliers in 1950). The complete overhaul of the theatre by the Stoll Moss group and designer Carl Toms in the 1980s, resulted in a larger stage, a reconstitution of much of the earlier ambience, and a thorough cleaning, leaving the stone facade and interior gleaming. At the entrance, the 1930 mural of nude chorus girls has been retained.

Anton Dolin and Dora Vadimova were among the clothed dancers in *Charlot's Masquerade*, the opening production, which also featured Beatrice Lillie, Florence Desmond and Henry Kendall. France was well represented in the first years by seasons of Sacha Guitry (1932) and the Comedie Française (1934), but the English contingent failed to make a go of the theatre, and it became a venue for trade film shows in the late 1930s. The war years brought it back into circulation with Edith Evans, Robert Donat and Isabel Jeans in Shaw's *Heartbreak House* (1943), and Johann Strauss' operetta *A Night In Venice* (1944). In 1946, Jan Pomeroy founded the New London Opera Company, which made the Cambridge its home for two years before moving to Sadler's Wells. Opera and ballet seemed particularly suitable for the large house of 1275 seats. Menotti's opera *The Consul* had its British premiere here with a mainly American cast, and Peter Daubeny presented seasons of foreign dance companies between 1951 and 1952. Previously, there were two popular revues, *Sauce Tartare* (1949) and *Sauce Piquante* (1950),

The decorative foyer frieze designed by Carl Toms for the refurbished Cambridge Theatre

Maggie Smith starred as Hedda Gabler *(1970) in a revelatory production by Ingmar Bergman*

the latter having a 21-year-old unknown named Audrey Hepburn in the chorus.

Straight plays returned to the Cambridge in 1952 with *Affairs Of State* starring Joyce Redman, Coral Browne, Hugh Williams, Basil Radford and Wilfrid Hyde-White for 18 months. An even longer run was clocked up by William Douglas Home's *The Reluctant Debutante* (1955), a typically pre-'kitchen sink' drawing room comedy. In 1960, ripples of the New Wave were felt at the Cambridge with John Mortimer's first full-length play, *The Wrong Side Of The Park*, with Margaret Leighton and Robert Stephens; and 24-year-old Albert Finney was Keith Waterhouse and Willis Hall's *Billy Liar*. Other successes of the period were Margaret Lockwood in *Signpost To Murder* (1962); Tommy Steele as Kipps in the British musical *Half A Sixpence* (1963), which earned considerably more than the title; and Bruce Forsyth playing seven roles in the American musical *Little Me* (1964).

In September 1965, Ingrid Bergman, Michael Redgrave and Emlyn Williams triumphed in Turgenev's *A*

Ingrid Bergman and Michael Redgrave in A Month In The Country *(1965)*

'The Cambridge Theatre . . . originally decorated with amusing Jazz Age motifs by Serge Chermayeff, is now covered in dull ox-blood paint.'

Simon Tidworth, *Theatres*, 1973

Month In The Country, the Redgrave production that had opened the new Yvonne Arnaud Theatre in Guildford a few months earlier. But the prestige this generated did not sustain the theatre for too long, and a number of flops forced it to become a cinema for six months from September 1967. Then, in 1968, tenor John Hanson rode to the rescue as the Red Shadow in *The Desert Song*, and *The Student Prince*, old-fashioned productions of old-time Sigmund Romberg operettas, which found an audience.

A very different audience converged on the Cambridge in 1970 for the National Theatre Company season, the highlights of which were Maggie Smith in Ingmar Bergman's production of *Hedda Gabler*, and

The new foyer ceiling at the Cambridge. The rebuilding is extensive and, by summer of 1987, the auditorium and exterior were still under scaffolding

Laurence Olivier's Shylock in Jonathan Miller's 19th-century updating of *The Merchant Of Venice*. Quality was maintained in 1971, which saw contrasting Hamlets from Alan Bates and Ian McKellen, the return of Ingrid Bergman in Shaw's *Captain Brassbound's Conversion*, and Ralph Richardson and Jill Bennett in John Osborne's *West Of Suez*. But a number of duds and transfers had the Cambridge floundering again until two archetypal British farces – *Two And Two Make Sex* (1973) and *A Bit Between The Teeth* (1974) – brought business back. Michael Denison was the only white performer in *The Black Mikado* (1975), which ran for nearly two years; the all-black *Ipi Tombi* (1977) was also a hit; the all-white Joan Collins, dressed to the nines, ambled glamorously through *The Last Mrs Cheyney* (1981); and Peter O'Toole scored as John Tanner in Shaw's *Man And Superman* (1982) before the theatre re-emerged, in late 1987, with a brightened-up facade to face the future.

THE COLISEUM

One of the most eye-catching landmarks of the West End is the spinning globe of the Coliseum, dominating St Martin's Lane. The colourful sphere tops off an enormous square tower with solid columns, bold carved figures at each end representing Art, Music, Science and Literature, and a pride of sculptured lions. Today, the globe, lit from within to give the impression of movement, is the beckoning sign for opera lovers – London's largest theatre has been the home of the prestigious and enterprising English National Opera Company since 1974.

This grandiose Edwardian edifice was the dream child of the great theatre manager Oswald Stoll. An Australian of Irish parentage, he found himself, on the death of his stepfather, running the family's music hall in Liverpool at the tender age of 14. Stoll was soon controlling an extensive chain of halls throughout the country. In Victorian times, the music hall, whose origin lay in the entertainments at taverns in the 18th century, had a bawdy and boisterous reputation. Stoll planned to build a theatre where a man could bring his family without fear of shocking them.

The imposing playhouse with its Italian Renaissance style facade, designed by the renowned Frank Matcham, leading theatre architect of the day, opened its doors on 24 December, 1904. Crowds flocked out of curiosity to see the palace of pleasures as much as from any desire to attend the four-show-a-day variety programme. The latter contained such delights as 'The American Sisters Meredith' singing Oowana, an Indian love song, Madge Lessing accompanied by a troop of Highland soldiers with pipe band, and a Derby finale in which real horses were ridden on the huge revolving stage, the first such in Great Britain.

Norman Bailey (centre) as Hans Sachs in the 1986 revival of Wagner's The Mastersinger, *with Kathryn Harries as Eva*

A lively scene from Offenbach's Orpheus in the Underworld, *in a colourful production specially designed by cartoonist Gerald Scarfe in 1985*

In the first week, 67,000 people came to marvel at the mosaic and marble walls and ceilings, elaborate Grand Salon and Grand Staircase, and 'the only theatre in Europe which provides lifts to take the audience to the upper parts of the building . . . primarily for elevation to the handsome Terrace Tea Room,' as an early programme sheet proclaimed. (The roof garden was pulled down in 1951.) But the novelty of the structure soon wore off, and the shows were not sufficiently good to continue drawing the crowds. By expunging the more ribald elements and substituting decorous spectacles, Stoll lost the working and lower middle-class audiences that were the mainstay of music hall. 'Coarseness and vulgarity are not allowed at the Coliseum,' read an unenticing advertisement.

In an attempt to revitalize the box-office, Stoll presented *The Revue* in 1906, 'invented and produced' by Victor de Cottens of the Folies Bergère in Paris. The commère (female compère) was 20-year-old Billie Burke, who was to marry Florenz Ziegfeld, the master of the American revue, seven years later. Despite its success, the 300-cast show cost Stoll a fortune to mount, and he was forced to close the theatre in June of the same year. It remained dark until December 1907, when the globe lit up the London skyline again. Stoll returned, having formed a new syndicate, cut the four shows a day by half, and tempted in the great names of

the music hall who had previously been put off by the theatre's earlier slogan of *Pro Bono Publico* (For the Public Good). From 1909 to 1931, the 2358-seat auditorium was packed to the rafters by crowds enjoying such legendary entertainers as Harry Lauder, Little Tich, Harry Tate, Albert Chevalier, Nellie Wallace, and male impersonator Vesta Tilley. These acts were interspersed with performing animals, jugglers, acrobats, and curiosities like Fräulein Brunnhilde, 'the tallest pianist in the world' at seven-foot eleven. Who would have predicted that Wagner's Brunnhilde would appear on the same stage one day?

When Stoll invited Sergei Diaghilev to bring his Russian Ballet to the Coliseum after their sensational visit to Paris in 1909, the famed impresario said, 'The Russian Ballet sandwiched between performing dogs and a fat lady playing a silver-plated trombone! Never! Never!' However, his troupe did leap the boards of the Coliseum in 1917 after their brilliant pre-war period. In fact, it was not unusual for stars of the 'legitimate' theatre to appear between 'performing dogs and a fat lady'. Ellen Terry played Portia in the trial scene from *The Merchant Of Venice* in 1918, Lily Langtry paid

> *'In between the matinee and evening
> performance, the Coliseum stage appeared
> vaster and more mysterious, like an empty,
> echoing cathedral smelling faintly of dust.'*
>
> Noel Coward

two glowing visits in 1917 and 1918, and Sarah Bernhardt appeared each year between 1910 and 1913. Her last visit in 1916 was after the amputation of her leg forced her to perform sitting down. Opera was first staged here in 1912 when the Beecham Opera Company presented *Hansel And Gretel,* but was not to return for some years.

Despite a range of dazzling artists including Jack Buchanan, Gertrude Lawrence, Beatrice Lillie, Jack Hulbert, Cicely Courtneidge and Ronald Colman from England; Marie Dressler, Helen Morgan, W. C. Fields and the Marx Brothers from the USA, by 1931 variety was no longer the spice of live theatre. It was time for the Coliseum to change direction. In April, a new policy was instituted with the opening of *White Horse Inn.* The size of the auditorium, never kind to straight theatre, proved ideal for musical comedy, which held centre stage in the theatre's history for the next three decades. *White Horse Inn,* which ran for 651 per-

formances, was followed by *Casanova* in the same lavish vein. Other large scale productions included a 'real ice' spectacle called *St Moritz* in 1937.

During World War II the theatre remained open, bringing cheer to besieged Londoners. It was twice hit by incendiary bombs, but only minor damage was done. In January 1942, Sir Oswald Stoll (he was knighted in 1919) died aged 76. The theatre was bought by Prince Littler who revived *White Horse Inn, Me And My Girl, Maid Of The Mountains, The Belle Of New York,* and *The Merry Widow.* But on 7th June, 1947 *Annie Get Your Gun* proved that anything the West End could do in musical comedy, Broadway could do better. The energetic, witty and tuneful Irving Berlin show burst onto the London stage, running for three years, the longest in this theatre's history. *Kiss Me Kate*

Opera-goers fill the beautiful Matcham-designed auditorium

Jonathan Miller set Gilbert and Sullivan's The Mikado *in 1920s England. Heroine Yum-Yum and her friends were lacrosse-playing schoolgirls. It was a smash-hit for the ENO in 1986/87*

(1951), *Call Me Madam* (1952), *Guys And Dolls* (1953), *Can Can* (1954), *The Pyjama Game* (1955), *Damn Yankees, Bells Are Ringing* (both 1957) and *The Most Happy Fella* (1960), proved that the Broadway musical was here to stay.

Sadly, because two of the greatest Broadway musicals, *My Fair Lady* and *West Side Story,* with better casts, were occupying Drury Lane and Her Majesty's respectively, the Coliseum found it increasingly difficult to compete. In 1961, MGM, sniffing around for a large theatre in which to instal Cinerama equipment, took a long lease on the building, turning it into a cinema. As the widest of wide screen processes needed three massive projectors to be placed at the back of the stalls, extensive alterations were done to the auditorium. It remained a none-too-successful enterprise until MGM decided not to renew the lease in 1967.

Meanwhile, Sadler's Wells Opera was beginning to find its theatre in Islington too small and too far from the West End. Stephen Arlen, managing director of the company, entered into negotiations with Prince Littler, and took a 10-year lease. A great deal had to be done to repair the damage caused by the Cinerama misadventure in order to achieve the warm, welcoming, comfortable opera house, with superb acoustics, that we know today. This vastly successful venture has introduced a whole new generation to opera in less elitist and stuffy confines than the Royal Opera House – and at cheaper prices. In each 10-month season, more than 20 works are given, and often four different operas can be seen in a week.

Their policy has been, from the opening production of *Don Giovanni* on 21 August, 1968, to perform a wide range of operas, including new works, all in English. Apart from their achievements in the classics of the operatic repertoire, such as a complete and impressive *Ring* cycle, they have tackled many less familiar operas of merit. Prokofiev's *The Gambler* and his spectacular *War And Peace,* Tchaikovsky's *Mazeppa,* Martinu's *Julietta* and Wagner's *Rienzi* are examples of the latter. Proving that opera is a living art form, contemporary works have included Ligeti's *Le Grand Macabre* and Philip Glass's *Akhnaten,* while a new slant was given to more traditional operas as in Jonathan Miller's brilliant New York Mafia *Rigoletto,* and his production of *The Mikado* with an English 20s setting. In 1974, the Sadler's Wells Opera was renamed the English National Opera under the managing directorship of Lord Harewood, the Queen's cousin and a dedicated and knowledgeable opera lover whose worthy successor since 1986 is Peter Jonas. As Harewood wrote in 1980, the Coliseum 'combines the sometimes opposing attributes of style and unpretentiousness, beauty and the sort of familiarity which quickly makes one feel at home.'

THE COMEDY

'Panton Street in the Haymarket has for very many years past enjoyed a dubious reputation owing to the numerous "night-houses" once existing in this vicinity. Recent improvements in this and the adjacent thoroughfares have now removed altogether the doubtful resorts of the roisterers of other days, and the demolition of a large pile of buildings on the south side has enabled a spacious theatre to be constructed which seems likely to take a prominent place among the West End establishments devoted to public amusement.' So wrote *The Daily Telegraph* on 14 October, 1881 on the opening of the Comedy Theatre.

Today, there are still plenty of 'roisterers' and 'doubtful resorts' in nearby Soho, but the Comedy is coyly tucked away from the hurly-burly in a quiet side street. On visiting it, one enters the past. The pedimented classical facade, with its Greek 'Lady with the Lamp' sculpture above the entrance, is virtually the same as when it was conceived by Thomas Verity over a century

ago, but for the addition of a modern wrought iron canopy. Built in a record time of six months, the building also has one of the few extant pre-1890 auditoria in London, despite some alterations along the way. This has its disadvantages: pillars still hold up the Dress Circle (paradoxically, at ground level), obscuring the view from certain seats, and the stage is the smallest of any theatre of comparable size in London. The dominant colour of the French Renaissance decor – from the exquisite ceiling to the wallpaper – is gold. Many of its productions, too, have been pure gold, with a fair portion of dross in between.

The Comedy's first manager, Alexander Henderson, intended the venue as a house of comic opera to rival Gilbert and Sullivan's Savoy Theatre, which had opened only five days earlier. The première production was an English version of Edmond Audran's French op-

The Comedy bar

'The architect Sir John Summerson wrote that the Comedy Theatre was the best and most originally preserved of London theatres, and I must say that I agree with him.'

Sir Ralph Richardson

eretta, *The Mascotte.* Similar works followed, some of them featuring Violet Melnotte (born Rosenberg in Birmingham), who took over the Comedy for a while before moving into the Trafalgar Square Theatre (later the Duke Of York's) in 1892. In 1887, Herbert Beerbohm Tree had his first big success as actor-manager with *The Red Lamp,* which he later transferred to the Haymarket when he took over the management there. Another legendary figure of the age, Sarah Bernhardt, appeared in Sardou's *Tosca* and *Fédora,* roles written with her in mind.

In the last decade of the century, managers and plays came and went until Lewis Waller, one of the outstanding romantic actors of the day, rescued the theatre from the doldrums by presenting Booth Tarkington's *Monsieur Beaucaire* (1902), with himself in the title role, for 430 performances. The equally romantic 23-year-old John Barrymore made his first London appearance in *The Dictator* (1905), while the following year E. W. Hornung's *Raffles,* coincidentally played by Barrymore in a 1917 silent film, started the Edwardian craze for 'crook' plays. The glamorous Gerald du Maurier (father of novelist Daphne) portrayed the dapper gentleman burglar, altering tradition by turning the villain into the hero. Somerset Maugham, the darling of the West End, had three plays performed at the Comedy between 1908 and 1911. They starred Marie Tempest (who made her debut here in *Boccaccio,* 1895) in *Mrs Dot* and *Penelope,* and Marie Löhr in *Smith.*

During World War I, Laurette Taylor re-created her New York triumph here in her husband John Hartley Manners' play *Peg O' My Heart* (1914) for 710 performances. Six revues then occupied the stage until the end of the war, produced by the kings of revue, Albert de Courville, C. B. Cochran and André Charlot. It was in Charlot's *Tails Up* (1918), starring Jack Buchanan, that Noel Coward's name first appeared in the West End as a lyric writer. Revues continued as a significant part of the Comedy's programmes for the next few decades. Douglas Byng was in *How D'You Do?* (1933) and *Hi Diddle-Diddle* (1934), the two Hermiones (Gingold and Baddeley) in *Rise Above It* (1941), Gingold in *Slings And Arrows* (1948); there was the Flanders and Swann *Fresh Airs* (1956), 23-year-old Maggie Smith's West End debut in *Share My Lettuce* (1957) and *The Premise* (1962), an American revue which relied on improvization.

The Comedy certainly lived up to its name, and dramas were not the theatre's strong point. Then, in 1956, the theatre played a vital part in helping to undermine the archaic censorship laws of Britain. Until 1968, the unlamented Lord Chamberlain had the right to ban plays if the subject or language was deemed unsuitable. Since it was forbidden to portray homosexuality (or even the suggestion of it), a group of West End managers got together to form The New Watergate Club at the Comedy where they could present banned plays under club conditions. By paying a five-shilling subscription, audiences were able to see three American plays refused a license: Arthur Miller's *A View From The Bridge* (1956), Robert Anderson's *Tea And Sympathy* (1957), and Tennessee Williams' *Cat On*

The finely detailed auditorium ceiling

Joe Melia and Zena Walker administer to their totally handicapped 'vegetable' child in Peter Nichols' powerful tragi-comedy, A Day In The Death Of Joe Egg

Barry James and Ellen Greene cower in front of the plant 'monster' in Little Shop Of Horrors

A Hot Tin Roof (1958). Some time later the Lord Chamberlain's office admitted that homosexuality 'is now so widely debated, written about and talked over that its complete exclusion from the stage can no longer be regarded as justifiable.' The club, therefore, became unnecessary.

The newly-gained concession allowed Peter Shaffer's first play, *Five Finger Exercise,* with its subtle homosexual thread, to enjoy a two-year commercial run from 1958. The passing of both time and the Lord Chamberlain brought male and female nudity to the same theatre in the prison drama, *Fortune And Men's Eyes,* and in Nell Dunn's long-running *Steaming* (1980), set in a women's Turkish bath. Other controversial productions included Peter Nichols' *A Day In The Death Of Joe Egg* (1967), Christopher Hampton's *Savages* (1973) starring Paul Scofield, and David Hare's *Knuckle* (1974) with Edward Fox. Two successful 'horror musicals', *The Rocky Horror Show* (1979) and *Little Shop Of Horrors* (1983) shook the Victorian foundations of the Comedy, but left its delightful structure still standing and entertainment within still flourishing.

THE CRITERION

Opposite the beautifully-cleaned statue of Eros at Piccadilly Circus stands the rather grimy and neglected Second Empire-style, 1873 facade of the old Criterion Restaurant building. Next to the White Bear Inn, which has retained the name of the 17th-century posting inn that stood on the site, a tiny, unnoteworthy entrance leads into one of London's most entrancing and historically important theatres.

Apart from the vestibule (where hangs a full-length portrait of actress-manager Mary Moore), the entire theatre, as conceived by Thomas Verity, is underground. To reach the almost perfectly preserved mid-Victorian auditorium, one descends a flight of stairs between striking tiled walls painted with classical figures, muses, and the names of famous composers. The mini maze of corridors, large mirrors, and ceilings adorned with cherubs on clouds, gives audiences a feeling of space to counteract any claustrophobia. . . . Indeed, for 10 years after the opening in 1874 – until the building was enlarged and properly ventilated – it was necessary to pump air into the theatre to prevent the public from suffocating.

It is easy to imagine, when seated and waiting for the curtain to rise, lovely bejewelled ladies and their Victorian toff escorts surrounded by the pink-and-aubergine decor of the stalls, or leaning forward on the curved-front boxes. In the Royal Box, still used for royalty and VIPs, one might have spotted the Prince of Wales applauding his mistress Lily Langtry, appearing opposite Charles Wyndham in *The Fringe Of Society* (1892). If they could be brought back to life, they would still recognise the house, but might be a trifle disturbed by the plays. After all, there were gasps of horror when Kate Rorke, playing a rebellious girl in *Fourteen Days*, lit up a cigarette.

What audiences would have seen and enjoyed in 1877 was a French farce, adapted by James Albery, called *Pink Dominoes*. In the cast was Charles

49

'The Criterion Theatre, transformed from a stuffy band-box to a convenient, handsome and well-ventilated house . . .'

Dramatic Notes, 1884

Wyndham, who took over the theatre in 1879 and whose initials are seen in decorative monograms on the walls. Enter Albery's wife, Mary Moore (billed as Miss M. Mortimer), making her first appearance here in *The Candidate* (1884). A woman of great beauty and intelligence, she soon became Wyndham's leading lady (they married in 1916) in such roles as Lady Amaranthe in John O'Keefe's *Wild Oats* and Ada Ingot in Tom Robertson's *David Garrick* (both 1886). A year later the future King Edward VII invited them to give a command performance of the latter play at Sandringham.

Although the theatre gained a reputation for light comedy, it was Arthur Henry Jones' dramas of social criticism that claimed the attention in the last years of the century, notably *The Bauble Shop* (1893), *The Case Of Rebellious Susan* (1894) and *The Liars* (1897). In 1899, Wyndham left to go to the theatre that bears his name. He returned eight years later with a production of Hubert Henry Davies' *The Mollusc*, in which Mary Moore's performance was a *tour de force*, although she barely stirred from a settee throughout. From 1915 to 1919, running almost as long as World War I, was a farce entitled *A Little Bit Of Fluff*, of which Lynton Hudson in *The English Stage 1850-1950* commented that although 'its illusory suggestion of naughtiness – and one solitary and by modern standards entirely decorous glimpse of a silk-clad shapely leg – dominated the war-time theatre, it would be unfair to blame the innocents who enjoyed this light-hearted fare for a deterioration in public taste.' Its run of 1241 performances has only been surpassed here by Ray Cooney's *Run For Your Wife!* (1983).

Cyril Maude in *Lord Richard In The Pantry* (1919),

Up the stairway to the foyer (right) and the beautiful tiled and mirrored hallway (below)

Nora, the heroine of Ibsen's A Doll's House, *and her husband Torvald, were brought brilliantly to life by Claire Bloom and Colin Blakely in 1973*

Charles Hawtrey in *Ambrose Applejohn's Adventure* (1921), Sybil Thorndike in *Advertising April* (1923), and Marie Tempest in five plays between 1926 to 1929, enlivened the rather scanty comedies, and brought in the public. At the death of Mary Moore in 1931, her son Bronson Albery took over the running of the theatre. He presented John Gielgud in *Musical Chairs* (1932) by the young and talented Ronald MacKenzie, who was killed in a car crash after the play had been running a year. In 1936, 24-year-old Terence Rattigan's *French Without Tears* started its three-year run, making its author rich and famous. Lesley Storm's comedy, *Tony Draws A Horse* was the last pre-war success.

During World War II, the Criterion proved to be a

Percy Mtwa and Mbongeni Ngema in the biting satire on South Africa, Woza Albert *(1983)*

The ornate, pillared auditorium

perfect underground shelter for a BBC studio to beam light entertainment to the nation. It was from here that the wartime radio hit ITMA (It's That Man Again) was broadcast. As soon as peace was declared, the theatre opened its doors for business again with Edith Evans a delightful Mrs Malaprop in *The Rivals* (1945). For the next 10 years, the Criterion offered a number of profitable comedies including *The Guinea Pig* (1946), in which the expression 'kick up the arse' caused audiences to fall about; Gladys Cooper varying her lines from night to night in Peter Ustinov's *The Indifferent Shepherd* (1948), and Rattigan's *Who Is Sylvia?* (1950).

A very different kind of play, Samuel Beckett's modern classic, *Waiting For Godot* (1955), surprised everybody by running a year. At one particular performance, when an old bearded gentleman made his way belatedly to his seat, a cry from the gallery went up that Godot had arrived at last. Jean Anouilh's *The Waltz Of The Toreadors* (1956) followed for a long run. Both these plays were directed by 25-year-old Peter Hall, who had transferred them from the Arts Theatre Club. A couple of other 'avant garde' productions were *Three* (1961), a triple bill of plays by Harold Pinter, John Mortimer and

N. F. Simpson, and James Saunders' *Next Time I'll Sing To You* (1962) with an unknown Michael Caine in the cast. More conventional hits were the marital comedies, *The Irregular Verb To Love* (1961) with Joan Greenwood, *A Severed Head* (1963), adapted by J. B. Priestley and Iris Murdoch from the latter's novel, and Alan Ayckbourn's *Absurd Person Singular* (1973). In between, Simon Gray's acerbic *Butley* (1971), starring Alan Bates, kept the theatre full. Among the few flops was a revue called *Hulla Baloo* (1972), set in a 'loo', with contributions from two young men named Andrew Lloyd Webber and Tim Rice – not something they would now wish to remember.

In the few years before the farce *Run For Your Wife!* began its 1600 and more performances, quality productions included Ibsen's *A Doll's House* (1973), with Claire Bloom repeating her Broadway triumph, *Bent* (1978), and Dario Fo's *Can't Pay, Won't Pay* (1981). The Criterion's subterranean location has its disadvantages, being particularly susceptible to damp. Forty-five thousand pounds was spent on improvements in 1972, and in 1985 the theatre suffered extensive flood damage which ruined some of its unique tiles. Happily, it has nonetheless survived and continues to give pleasure to playgoers.

THE DOMINION

'In the opinion of the Board, the most popular form of entertainment today consists of musical productions, which must be staged on so lavish a scale and be of such magnificence that a theatre with a very large seating capacity is required to render the production commercially successful, and there is undoubtedly a large public demand for big spectacular musical productions at popular prices with high class artistes.' This extract from a report on the building of 'A New Super-Theatre in the Centre of London' could easily have been written in 1987 when 'big spectacular musical productions' were booming. It was, however, issued in February 1928, just before construction began on the 2800-seat Dominion Theatre, which stands on the busy intersection of Tottenham Court Road and Oxford Street.

For many years, the Dominion was used as a cinema, or temporary home for short seasons of opera, dance and rock until it re-entered the mainstream of West End theatres with its production of the Dave Clark space-age musical *Time* (1986). But it opened as a theatre in October 1929 with an American musical comedy on golf by De Sylva, Brown and Henderson called *Follow Through* (*Follow Thru* on Broadway) starring Elsie Randolph, Ivy Tresmand and Leslie Henson. Neither this, nor a follow-up musical, *Silver Wings*, made much impression. So, in 1930, it provided a venue for Lon Chaney's *The Phantom Of The Opera* with 35% dialogue and some new footage added to the 1925 silent movie. The next year, Charlie Chaplin appeared on stage to make a 'thank you' speech after the first showing of his *City Lights*, in the presence of George V. The screen was folded up in 1932 to

The large, cinema-style foyer

allow Richard Tauber to move his ample form, from which emanated his dulcet tenor tones, in a revival of Franz Lehar's *The Land Of Smiles*. A number of film stars, including Maurice Chevalier, Jeanette Mac-Donald, Sophie Tucker and Judy Garland, made appearances in variety seasons.

In 1958, Todd-AO equipment was installed for the showing of the movie musical *South Pacific* which ran four years, a record surpassed by *The Sound Of Music*, which resounded through the Dominion from 1965 to 1973. For over a decade thereafter, blockbuster films shared the auditorium with the Welsh National Opera, the Georgian dancers from the USSR, Chinese acro-

The Georgian State Dance Company, one of many international events at the Dominion, in Samaya *(1985)*

'At first sight the interior of the house gives one the impression it was really meant for a super cinema.'

The Stage, 1929

bats, and pop groups. In a way, this was reminiscent of the days when there was a fun fair and a huge tent where variety shows were given, on the empty site on which the Dominion was built. Long before, as far back as the 12th century, the St Giles Leper Hospital had stood on the spot. Some six centuries later, a brewery was built here containing a 22-foot vat of porter ale. In October 1814, the vat burst, pouring its contents into the streets and literally drowning eight people in alcohol.

The site was chosen for the theatre 'owing to its central position, its proximity to the reconstructed Tube station.' Designed by W. and T. R. Milburn, its broad Portland stone facade is now obscured by a giant sign announcing the entertainment within. The interior, with its large mirrored lobby, twin stairways and wide

A characteristic scene from the 'space-age' musical, Time

corridors is very much on the lines of 'the modern picture palaces' built in the 30s. In order to accommodate *Time*, one of the most expensive stage musicals ever, a few alterations have had to be made.

'*Time* at the Dominion is a giant of a show in the size of its technical wizardry,' wrote the *Daily Telegraph* critic. Much of the 'technical wizardry' was achieved by a large dish fitted with revolving lights placed on the ceiling. The front of the circle was knocked out to provide room for three projectors to create the gigantic hologram of Sir Laurence Olivier, as a god who emerges from a huge egg to act as mentor to 'The Rock Star'. Casts may come and go, but Sir Laurence's image will last till the end of *Time*. Although the theatre still has a movie projector, screen and sound equipment ready to be hauled out again if necessary, the slogan of *Time* reads, 'In the beginning there was Time, now Time is a beginning.'

DRURY LANE, THE THEATRE ROYAL

It is ironic that London's oldest, most historically important, and most famous theatre, does not echo to the sounds of Shakespeare or other great English playwrights, but to the lusty melodies of the Broadway musical. For the last 40 years, since *Oklahoma* wowed British audiences in 1947, Drury Lane's large stage and 2283 seating capacity has housed the best of American musicals including *Carousel* (1950), *South Pacific* (1951) starring Mary Martin (her son Larry 'J. R.' Hagman was in the chorus), *The King And I* (1953), the record-breaking *My Fair Lady* (1958) with Rex Harrison and Julie Andrews, *Camelot* (1964), Carol Channing in *Hello Dolly!* (1965), Ginger Rogers making a triumphant comeback as *Mame* (1969), *A Chorus Line* (1976), *Sweeney Todd* (1980),*The Best Little Whore-*

house In Texas (1981), and *42nd Street* (1984). In fact, Americans have found it cheaper to see a hit musical here than on Broadway. Indeed, for most of its 324 years of existence (in four different buildings on the same spot), the name of Drury Lane has been synonymous with popular, spectacular shows, not dissimilar from what Broadway musicals are all about.

The first playhouse was erected on the site of a riding yard in 1662, two years after the Restoration. The theatre-loving Charles II granted a Patent to the company, under Thomas Killigrew, known as The King's Servants. As they were considered part of the Royal Household, the members of the troupe were entitled to wear the scarlet and gold of the Royal livery, and this is still worn by the footmen at Drury Lane

The renowned David Garrick as Tancred *(painted by Thomas Worlidge)*

today. The entire theatre, seating around 700, was about the size of the present stage. Refreshments were supplied by Mrs Mary Meggs, or 'Orange Moll', a widow who had a licence to hawk her fruits to all customers, except those in the upper gallery who might be inclined to throw them at some unfortunate player. One of 'Moll's' girls, Nell Gwynn, made her stage debut at the age of 15 in John Dryden's *The Indian Queen* in 1665. The King, from the Royal Box, fell in love with Nell at first sight, and took her as his mistress. It is likely that the fire that destroyed the building in 1672 was started by an 'orange girl' searching for fruit with a naked flame under the stairs where it was kept.

Sir Christopher Wren, the supreme architect of St Paul's Cathedral, designed the second theatre, the foundations of which can still be traced under the present stage. It was more than twice the size of the first, and prospered with the plays of Dryden, William Wycherley, William Congreve and George Farquhar, the cream of Restoration dramatists. After the deaths of Killigrew and Good King Charles, the Theatre Royal's prestige suffered until the triumvirate of Robert Wilkes, Thomas Doggett and Colley Cibber, all three fine actors, restored its fortunes in 1711. When Charles Fleetwood, a gambler with no money sense, took over, the theatre was led into near bankruptcy, despite an epoch-making *Merchant Of Venice* of 1741 in which Charles Macklin raised the role of Shylock from low comedy to a tragic figure. So impressive did George II find it, that he could not get to sleep either during or after the performance. Macklin was a forerunner of a new school of action which David Garrick was to personify.

Garrick, one of the greatest of English actors, became actor-manager in 1747, and spent the next 30 years of his career at Drury Lane. He introduced better lighting, regular rehearsals, and removed the public from the boxes on the sides of the stage. Garrick left the theatre in the hands of the celebrated playwright, Richard Brinsley Sheridan, whose first important production was his own *The School For Scandal* in 1777. Two years later, Sheridan's *The Critic* exploited the popular taste for spectacle with remarkable scenic effects and lavish costumes. He engaged the superb tragedienne Mrs Sarah Siddons to play Lady Macbeth, and her brother John Philip Kemble to make his London debut as Hamlet. However, by 1791, the building had fallen into such a bad state of decay that it was decided to build another in its place. So down went Wren's edifice, and up went one designed by Henry Holland, of which the *Morning Chronicle* of 1794 wrote, 'At length we have an English theatre worthy of our opulence and taste.' On the night of the opening production of *Macbeth,* with Kemble playing opposite his sister, an iron safety curtain was lowered to assure the audience of their protection from fire. Fifteen years later, the theatre burned down. Sheridan sat watching the conflagration with a glass of wine in his hand. When asked how he could do this so calmly, the playwright retorted, 'Can't a man have a drink by his own fireside?'

Drury Lane, more or less as we know it today, was rebuilt with money raised by the brewer Samuel Whitbread. Designed by Benjamin Wyatt on the elegant neo-classical model of the Grand Theatre of Bordeaux, it opened in 1812 with an address written by Lord Byron. Over the next few decades, several improvements were made. Gas lighting was introduced in 1817, the splendid portico was added in 1820, and the

'You are come to act in a wilderness of a place.'

Mrs Siddons to William Dowton in 1796

Actors gather in the Green Room, circa 1820

Russell Street colonnade in 1831. Certain things modern audiences take for granted, such as a centre aisle, stuffed and covered seats, and a coffee room, were much welcomed. The impressive Rotunda, magnificent Grand Salon and the sweeping staircases date from the early 19th century. It was on the latter that George III boxed the ears of his reprobate son, the

Prince Regent. This resulted in the staircases being called the King's Side and the Prince's Side, names still to be seen on opposite doors.

The new theatre, under the management of Samuel Arnold, introduced the legendary tragedian Edmund Kean to London audiences. He presented his Shylock, was immediately acclaimed a genius, and remained at Drury Lane, playing many of the great Shakespearean roles, for five years, his most successful part being Richard III. Of Kean's death scene as Richard, Hazlitt said he 'had a preternatural and terrific grandeur, as if his will could not be disarmed, and the very phantoms of his despair had a withering power.'

After Kean's departure, opera and spectacle were preferred to straight drama under the reign of Alfred Bunn. In 1879, Augustus Harris, a bronze bust of whom sits above a drinking fountain at the north-east corner of the facade, established the theatre's reputation for elaborately staged melodramas and pantomimes. When Harris, known as 'Druriolanus' died in

The great tragic actor Edmund Kean as Richard III

Dennis Quilley as the infamous demon barber, and Sheila Hancock as Mrs Lovett, the pie-shop proprietor, in Stephen Sondheim's Sweeney Todd

1896, his righthand man, Arthur Collins, continued the tradition with even bigger shows. *Ben Hur* (1902) offered a chariot race with real horses, and other productions contained earthquakes, erupting volcanos and shipwrecks. Sensation was piled on sensation, and the public flocked. Drury Lane was also the home for Henry Irving's last season in 1905, Ellen Terry's stage jubilee a year later, in which all the leading theatrical personalities of the day appeared at a mammoth matinee, and Diaghilev's landmark Ballet Russes. Shakespeare's Tercentenary in 1916 was celebrated with a production of *Julius Caesar,* after which Frank Benson, who took the title role, was knighted by George V with a property sword in the Royal retiring room.

After 27 years in the job, Collins handed over to Sir Alfred Butt in 1924, who instigated the policy of big musical shows from the USA such as *Rose Marie* (1925), *The Desert Song* (1927), *Show Boat* (1928) and *The New Moon* (1929). Franz Lehar's *Land Of Smiles* (1931), featuring Austrian-born tenor Richard Tauber, gave way to Noel Coward's patriotic pageant, *Cavalcade,* which ended with the 250-strong company singing the National Anthem and the audience, on its feet, joining in. The multi-talented Ivor Novello dominated

Drury Lane in the 1930s as leading man, composer and writer of *Glamorous Nights, Careless Rapture* and *The Dancing Years,* each title aptly describing the sort of entertainment that the Theatre Royal provided and continues to provide. Novello, 'the handsomest man in England', also played the soldier-king in a spectacular revival of *Henry V.*

During World War II, 'The Lane' became the headquarters of ENSA, the organization set up to provide shows for the allied forces at home and abroad. In 1940, considerable damage was done to the upper circles by enemy bombs, an explosion rivalling those the theatre had supplied on stage. Restored to its former glory, it reopened to the public on 19 December, 1946 with Coward's musical *Pacific 1860* starring Mary Martin. It flopped and made way for the arrival of Rodgers and Hammerstein's *Oklahoma,* which ushered in the golden age of Broadway hit musicals. On 30 April 1958, *My Fair Lady* started its run of 2281 performances, making it the longest-running show in Drury Lane's history.

Audiences that come to Drury Lane find themselves wandering around a veritable theatre museum before entering the auditorium. In the large foyer there is a statue of Shakespeare executed in lead by John Cheere.

Interval arrives in the grand auditorium of London's oldest theatre

'We're In The Money!'. One of the spectacular numbers from the long-running 42nd Street

On the walls behind are a handsome Patent Board with a list of all the holders since 1663, and a mahogany War Memorial with the names in gold of the members of the theatrical profession who fell in the Great War. In the Stalls and Circle Rotunda are statues and busts of Garrick, Kean, Novello, Dan Leno, Forbes-Robertson, and the first great black American actor Ira Aldridge, as well as a John Northcote painting of Kean as Brutus.

Like a few other old London theatres, Drury Lane has its resident ghosts. One, an 18th-century gentleman in long grey riding cloak, riding boots, sword and three-cornered hat, walks through one wall of the upper circle and disappears on the other side. But he only makes his appearance at matinees and when the house is full. He is thought to have some connection with the skeleton found bricked up in one of the walls with a dagger in his ribs. The other ghost, suspected of being that of the illustrious clown Grimaldi who made his farewell appearance at the theatre in 1828, gives bad actors a kick up the backside from time to time. As the standard of performance at Drury Lane is generally high, this is a rare event.

The statue of Edmund Kean blesses playgoers making their way to the stalls

THE DUCHESS

On the opposite side of Catherine Street from the grandiose Strand and the noble Drury Lane, is a small theatre seeking attention with its 'modern Tudor Gothic' facade. Three projecting bays with a plethora of tiny windows over enamelled panels bearing insignia, give it an elegant air which suits its name – the Duchess. Not much to catch the eye, though, in the unadorned two-level interior with its hidden lighting effect, enlivened only by two unusual *bas-reliefs* by the sculptor Maurice Lambert on each side of the stage. They represent draped figures holding the masks of Comedy and Tragedy above applauding hands. Over the years, hands have applauded plays by J.B. Priestley,

Emlyn Williams, Noel Coward and Harold Pinter . . . and *The Dirtiest Show In Town* and *Oh Calcutta*!

For most of its existence, the Duchess has been an intimate home for what Priestley called 'the essential Theatre . . . an institution that cannot safely be despised even by the philosopher.' Priestley, whose *Laburnum Grove* (1933) ran here for 335 performances, managed the threatre from 1934, the year in which two more plays of his were performed. Ralph Richardson, who would be closely associated with the works of Priestley, played an amiable drunkard in *Eden End*, and a businessman in *Cornelius*. 'I always see Ralph myself not as a down-to-earth character but as if he is

about to float away somewhere,' commented the playwright. Priestley's first play on the concept of time, *Time And The Conways* (1937) ran for over six months; after the war Sybil Thorndike starred in *The Linden Tree* (1947), while *Eden End* was revived (1948).

Emlyn Williams' links with the Duchess began as an actor in the opening production in November 1929 of a war play called *Tunnel Trench*. He returned as playwright and star in 1935 with *Night Must Fall*, the psychological thriller which contained the notorious head in the hatbox. His most popular play, *The Corn Is Green*, ran here from August 1938 until the theatre's closure at the outbreak of war in September 1939. Williams himself played the young Welsh miner who wins a scholarship to Oxford, thanks to his teacher Miss Moffat, a role taken brilliantly by Sybil Thorndike. In 1952, Williams brought his celebrated Dickens recital into the Duchess for a short season.

Although J. B. Priestley and Emlyn Williams were the dominant figures in the theatre's pre-war days, other notable productions were seen here. Nancy Price's People's National Theatre presented Baliol Holloway as Falstaff in *The Merry Wives Of Windsor* and Frank Vosper as Henry VIII in *The Rose Without A Thorn*, both in 1932. In the same year, Jessica Tandy scored a personal success in the all-female play, *Children In Uniform*, a translation from the German *Mädchen In Uniform*, set in an oppressive boarding school. It was directed by the Viennese Leontine Sagan, who had filmed it the year before.

During the war years, Noel Coward's 'impossible farce' *Blithe Spirit* (1942) continued to break records after being transferred here from the Piccadilly and the now defunct St James. In contrast, the shortest run in theatrical history was recorded at the Duchess in 1930 when a revue failed to complete the first night, the audience retreating before the end. Running considerably longer were post-war hits such as Wynyard Browne's *The Holly And The Ivy* (1950) and Terence Rattigan's drama *The Deep Blue Sea (1952)* with Peggy Ashcroft falling for feckless young Kenneth More, and attempting suicide. These dramas were examples of the 'well-made play', soon to be discarded by a new school of British writers, of whom Harold Pinter was one of

A bronze bas-relief *on either side of the proscenium is the only adornment*

'Ken Tynan had conceived a voyeurs' picnic . . . called Oh Calcutta! *. . . Mixing frontery with effrontery it soon found its own public.'*

Raymond Mander and Joe Mitchenson in *Revue*

Husky-voiced Joan Greenwood and fruity-toned Donald Sinden lent distinction to Terence Rattigan's In Praise Of Love *(1973)*

Vivien Merchant and Donald Pleasence in Harold Pinter's Tea Party *(1970), a teasing black comedy*

the best. Producer Michael Codron had the courage to bring Pinter's *The Caretaker* into the heart of the West End . . . and it paid off. This superb comedy of menace with a splendid cast of three – Donald Pleasence, Alan Bates (replaced by Pinter himself) and Peter Wood-thorpe – ran a year. Some years on, Pinter's double bill, *The Basement* and *The Tea Party* (1970) with Pleasence and Vivien Merchant (then the author's wife), and his triple bill, *Other Places* (1985), were seen in the vastly changed climate of British theatre.

Raunchy entertainment became the order of the day at the Duchess when it played hostess to *The Dirtiest Show In Town* (1971) for 794 performances, and the revue which merited the above title, *Oh Calcutta!* (1974) for six years. All of which seems to contradict the name of the comedy that continued its long run here: *No Sex Please We're British* (1986).

THE DUKE OF YORKS

This elegant, charming and compact Victorian playhouse was built in 1892, the first of the three theatres in St Martin's Lane – at the time literally a lane, with muddy ditches on either side. The New theatre (now the Albery) sprang up 11 years later, and the Coliseum soon joined them. With the Garrick backing onto the Duke of York's, and the Wyndham's close behind the Albery, they form a neat cluster of theatres between those in Shaftesbury Avenue and Drury Lane.

The Duke of York's opened as the Trafalgar Square Theatre, but changed to its present name in 1895 after Henry Dana, the manager, received the following letter from the treasurer of the future King George V. It read: 'I am desired to inform you that HRH the Duke of York has no objection to the Trafalgar Theatre being called The Duke of York's Theatre but to say that this permission gives no authority for the use of the word Royal in connexion *(sic)* with the theatre nor may any reference be made such as "By permission of HRH the Duke of York."' Nevertheless, it is a right royal building with a theatrical tradition fit for a king.

It was at the Duke of York's on 27 December, 1904 that *Peter Pan* flew for the first time on stage. Here, too, a year later, 14-year-old Charlie Chaplin played in *Sherlock Holmes.* On returning in the 1950s with his daughter, Victoria, to see a show, Chaplin was given the Royal Box with its Regency-inspired retiring room designed by Cecil Beaton. The theatre has also been graced over the years by, among others, Marie Tempest, Ellen Terry, Isadora Duncan, Edwige Feuillère, John Gielgud, Glenda Jackson and Al Pacino. Peggy Ashcroft (*Jew Süss,* 1929), John Mills (*London Wall,* 1931) and Joan Plowright (*Moby Dick,* 1955) all began to make their names here. Miss Plowright played the Cabin Boy to actor-director Orson Welles' Ahab in a production the critic Kenneth Tyan described as 'a sustained assault on the senses, which dwarfs anything London has ever seen since, perhaps, the Great Fire.' And. . .the theatre has its very own ghost.

An iron fire-door which once existed is heard to slam shut every night at ten. Some years ago, an old-fashioned iron key with a tag marked 'Iron Door' dropped at the feet of the manager. A female figure dressed in black has been seen to wander through the circle bar. It is said to be none other than the ghost of Violet Melnotte, the owner, known to everyone as 'Madame'. The theatre, designed by Walter Emden for

Pauline Chase as Peter Pan – one of J.M. Barrie's favourites in the role

'Madame' and her husband Frank Wyatt, was not a success until she let it on a long lease to the influential American impresario, Charles Frohman, in 1897. Frohman, 'The Napoleon of the Theatre', brought fame, prestige and money to the Duke of York's.

The first long run under his aegis was Anthony Hope's *The Adventure Of Lady Ursula* (1898) in which Evelyn Millard caused a stir by appearing in male attire. In 1900 she also starred in Jerome K. Jerome's *Miss Hobbs* and in David Belasco's one-act play, *Madame Butterfly,* that accompanied it. Puccini happened to be in the audience one evening, and was inspired to write his opera of the same name four years later. The long and fruitful collaboration between Frohman and James Barrie at the Duke of York's began with *The Admirable Crichton* (1902), a success despite a strike of scene-shifters after the second act on the opening night. Members of the cast, including H. B. Irving (son of Sir Henry), Gerald du Maurier and Irene Vanbrugh, had to move the scenery themselves. *Peter Pan* followed with Nina Boucicault, Hilda Trevelyan and du Maurier as

> *'Either he must be the whimsical fairy
> creature that Nina Boucicault made him, or
> he must be the lovable tomboy of Pauline
> Chase. There is no other way.'*

J.M. Barrie on the playing of Peter Pan

*The original Royal Retiring Room – alas, now
modernized – designed by Cecil Beaton*

the first ever Peter, Wendy and Hook respectively.
Cissie Loftus (1905), Pauline Chase (1906-1913) and
Madge Titheradge (1914) were the subsequent Peters
at this theatre. Hilda Trevelyan continued for some
years as Wendy, also proving herself a perfect Barrie
heroine in *Alice Sit-By-The-Fire* (1905), alongside
Ellen Terry, and as Maggie in *What Every Woman
Knows* (1908).

In 1910 Frohman made a brave attempt to mount a
repertory season of 10 plays, but suffered a heavy
financial loss. Among the plays premiéred were Galsworthy's *Justice,* Shaw's *Misalliance* and Granville-
Barker's *The Madras House.* Five years later, the
theatre world on both sides of the Atlantic was stunned
by the news that Frohman had drowned aboard the *S.S.
Lusitania,* torpedoed by the Germans. His last words to
a survivor were said to have been from *Peter Pan:* 'To
die will be an awfully big adventure.'

During the Great War, the theatre's successes were
Doris Keane in *Romance* (1915), Renée Kelly in *Daddy
Long Legs* (1916) and Mrs Patrick Campbell in *The
Thirteenth Chair* (1917). Noel Coward, in his 20s like
the century, became the voice of the Bright Young

Things. When he was 14, he had appeared as Slightly in
the 1913 *Peter Pan.* Now Coward was back with his revue, *London Calling:* (1923), in which Gertie Lawrence
sang 'Parisien Pierrot', and two plays, *Easy Virtue*
(1926) and *Home Chat* (1927). The latter, despite the
casting of two former Peter Pans, Nina Boucicault and
Madge Titheradge, was booed on the first night.
Coward's connection with the theatre re-emerged
years later with *Waiting In The Wings* (1960), featuring
a starry gerontological cast, and a 1963 revival of his
classic, *Private Lives.*

The 1930s ushered in the Carl Rosa Opera Company,
a non-stop season of Grand Guignol (from 2 p.m. to
midnight), and the Ballet Rambert and Markova-Dolin
dance companies which did so much to popularize ballet in England. The big hit of the 1940s was *Is Your
Honeymoon Really Necessary?* (1944), which ran two
years. Other long-runners were John Clements and
Kay Hammond in *The Happy Marriage* (1952), Flora
Robson in *The House By The Lake* (1956), Margaret
Lockwood in *And Suddenly It's Spring* (1959), which
had its 'first night' for the critics at a matinee; the Kenneth Williams revue, *One Over The Eight* (1961),
Donald Pleasence in Jean Anouilh's *Poor Bitos* (1964),
The Killing Of Sister George (1965), *Relatively Speak-*

*Joan Plowright and Orson Welles rehearse for
Moby Dick in 1955*

Glenda Jackson and Brian Cox in Eugene O'Neill's Strange Interlude. *They had to survive a marathon five hours per performance*

ing (1967) – the first of Alan Ayckbourn's multitude of hits – and *The Man Most Likely To . . .* (1970).

In 1979, Capital Radio bought the building and closed it for refurbishment. The fears of those who thought this diamond of a theatre would be ruined, were allayed on its re-opening in February 1980. The architects restored the original cream and gold decoration, recreating the warm atmosphere of a Victorian theatre, while improving the facilities. One significant improvement was the removal of the supporting pillars in the stalls which had obstructed the view from many a seat. The facade of painted brick and stone stays its aesthetic self, with its delightful first floor open loggia, balustrade and Ionic columns. The quality of productions have remained traditionally high, with Glenda Jackson in *Rose* (1980) and *Strange Interlude* (1983), Frances de la Tour in *Duet For One* (1980), the off-Broadway cast, headed by Al Pacino, in *American Buffalo* (1984) and the hit comedy *Stepping Out* (1985). Violet Melnotte can rest in peace.

THE FORTUNE

In the shadow of the glorious Drury Lane Theatre, facing its famous colonnade on the stage door side, lies a small theatre that proudly perpetuates the name of a popular Elizabethan playhouse. The architect, Ernest Schaufelberg, based his designs for the exterior on a print of doubtful authenticity of the old Fortune. Like its predecessor as seen in the sketch, it is a square brick building of four storeys, with minimal adornment. The earlier Fortune, situated not far from where the Barbican Centre stands today, had a statue of the Goddess of Fortune over the entrance. This proved rather ineffectual as the building, the costumes and playbooks went up in flames in 1621. Above the entrance of the present theatre is a nude figure of Terpsichore, the Greek Muse of Dancing. However, the small stage does not lend itself to any but limited displays of the art of dance. What the 440-seat theatre does provide is a cosy intimacy for shows of a diminutive nature. In fact, its biggest successes have been two revues – *At The Drop Of A Hat* (1957) and *Beyond The Fringe* (1961) – with casts of two and four respectively.

The Fortune's principal interest as a building is that it shares its structure with the Scottish National Church. Strangely, it is built over and under the church, whose entrance is cheek by jowl with that of the theatre's. The opening production in November 1924, a play called *Sinners* by Laurence Cowan, the theatre's owner, might have confused churchgoers. There have also been a few plays whose proximity could not have been welcomed by worshippers on the other side of the wall. Nevertheless, it is a rare architectural unity between religion and secularism.

A brass plate in the lobby proclaims, 'There is a tide in the affairs of men, which, taken at the flood, leads on to Fortune.' But, more often, it has been 'the slings and arrows of outrageous fortune' that have visited this pleasant playhouse. It was two years after its opening before there was anything significant to appeal to lovers of the theatre. The influential producer J. B. Fagan changed that by presenting Sean O'Casey's modern Irish classics, *Juno And The Paycock* and *The Plough And The Stars* in 1926. A year later the actor Tom Walls, at the time associated with the Aldwych farces, took over the management of the Fortune. Frederick Lonsdale's *On Approval* (1927), a comedy of manners about a trial marriage, ran for over a year, making it the first and last hit here for some time.

The People's National Theatre, run by Nancy Price, its founder and guiding spirit, found its first London home at the Fortune from 1930 to 1931. Their most noteworthy production was the revival of John Galsworthy's first play, *The Silver Box*. After Nancy Price – and her inseparable pet parrot – left the theatre, Sybil Thorndike paid a brief visit in 1932 with two plays. It was then given over to amateur productions until the war, during which it was used by ENSA, the organization formed to provide entertainment for servicemen and women.

After the war, the building was returned to the pro-

A 1920s programme cover depicts the proscenium of the then newly-built Fortune

'Our theatre was miscalled the Fortune . . . After a very short time we slid into the eternal obscurity of Fatal Fortune.'

Dirk Bogarde on the failure of *Power Without Glory*, 1947

fessional fold for a brief period. One of the short-lived productions was *Power Without Glory* (1947), a working class drama featuring two unknown actors named Kenneth More and Dirk Bogarde. It soon closed 'due to lack of star names on the canopy and the excessive competition from the energetic Americans across the street in *Oklahoma!*,' according to Bogarde. It was

another 10 years before fortune smiled on the little theatre with *At The Drop Of A Hat*. Michael Flanders in a wheelchair and Donald Swann at the piano entertained audiences with comic songs and patter for over two years.

In the autumn of 1961 a revue, written and performed on a bare stage by four young men just down

Dennis Lawson, Christina Matthews and – gagged – John Atterbury in Mr Cinders, *the delightful period musical revived in 1983*

from Oxbridge, took an emergent 'Swinging London' by storm. *Beyond The Fringe*, dubbed, in an unfortunate turn of phrase by critic Kenneth Tynan, 'the funniest revue that London has seen since the allies dropped the bomb on Hiroshima', was not only instrumental in starting the 'satire industry', but was the springboard for the exceptional future careers of Jonathan Miller, Peter Cook, Alan Bennett and Dudley Moore. The show ran 1,184 performances before transferring to the Mayfair in 1964.

Although *Wait A Minim* (1964), a South African revue; *The Promise* (1967) with Judi Dench and Ian McKellan; *Suddenly At Home* (1971), a thriller starring Penelope Keith; and transfers such as *Sleuth* (1973), *Mr Cinders* (1983), *Up 'n Under* (1984) and *Double Double* (1986) enjoyed respectable runs, major successes have otherwise eluded the Fortune. Yet, 'there is a tide. . .'

Formidable actress, Frances de la Tour, impersonated formidable writer, Lillian Hellman, in her one-woman show, Lillian, *in 1986*

THE GARRICK

If David Garrick, according to Dr Johnson, had added 'to the gaiety of nations' and 'the public stock of harmless pleasure', then so too has the attractive late Victorian playhouse named after the great 18th-century actor, and built exactly 110 years after his death. A copy of the lost Gainsborough portrait of Garrick beside a bust of Shakespeare welcomes one into the theatre at dress circle level. Cupids holding laurel-decked shields form part of the finely modelled plasterwork on the balcony fronts and, from the domed ornamental ceiling held up by caryatids above the boxes, hangs a chandelier. The gold leaf of the auditorium was restored in 1986 by the celebrated stage designer Carl Toms. At the same time, the distinctive Portland and Bath stone exterior, opposite the statue of Henry Irving, also had a flattering facelift, making the stately loggia colonnade at first floor level come up as good as new.

It was new in 1889 when Walter Emden and C. J. Phipps built it for actor-manager John Hare, with the money of W. S. Gilbert, earned from the light operas he wrote with Arthur Sullivan. The construction was delayed when the deep foundations hit an underground river known to the Romans. Today, underground trains run beneath the theatre. A new drama by Pinero entitled *The Profligate* with Hare, Forbes-Robertson, Lewis Waller and Katie Rorke, inaugurated the building in April 1889. Pinero's connection with the Garrick continued with *Lady Bountiful* (1891) and *The Notorious Mrs Ebbsmith* (1895), the latter living up to its title. During the run of the play, starring Mrs Patrick Campbell and John Hare, a woman bearing the name of Ebbsmith was found drowned in the Thames, a counterfoil of a ticket for the production in her pocket. Apparently, she had written to a friend that the play had preyed on her mind. In 1896, Hare (knighted in 1907) left the theatre where he had made such a success, particularly in the role of Benjamin Goldfinch in Sydney Grundy's *A Pair Of Spectacles* (1890), an adaptation from a French farce. In fact, from the latter to *When Did You Last See Your Trousers?* (1987), farce estab-

'The proscenium is created by the pilasters that frame the stage boxes; this was a dramatic and simple change.'

Victor Glasstone

lished itself at the Garrick as the dominant mode through a great deal of its history.

The new century began well for the Garrick when Arthur Bourchier and his wife Violet Vanbrugh leased it, beginning a splendid line of productions with J. M. Barrie's *The Wedding Guest* (1900). There followed Pinero's *Iris* (1901), Henry Arthur Jones' *Whitewashing Julia* (1903), Bourchier as Shylock in *The Merchant Of Venice* (1905), Henri Bernstein's *Samson* (1909), and *The Unwritten Law* (1911), a dramatisation of *Crime And Punishment*. Bourchier had an apartment at the top of the theatre with a staircase leading directly to the stage. It is known as the Phantom Staircase because Bourchier's ghost is said to descend it, sometimes slapping actors on the shoulder in friendly encouragement.

Another husband-and-wife management, Oscar Asche and Lily Brayton, packed the theatre for the 1911-1912 season in which Asche played Falstaff in *The Merry Wives Of Windsor*, and Hajj in *Kismet*. Other managements followed in quick succession, and no

discernible policy emerged until the 1940s. Between the wars, productions worth mentioning were Austin Page's *By Pigeon Post* (1918), *Cyrano De Bergerac* (1919), Seymour Hicks in *The Man In The Dress Clothes* (1922), Sutton Vane's allegorical drama *Outward Bound* (1923), and Ivor Novello in his own play, *The Rat* (1924). Somerset Maugham preferred to cast Olga Lindo as Sadie Thompson in *Rain* (1925) rather than the more exciting Tallulah Bankhead, who wanted the role. Five years later Tallulah did appear at the Garrick, as another tart with a heart of gold – Marguerite in *The Lady Of The Camellias*.

During a sparse period in the early 30s, the theatre even resorted to Old Time Music Hall until a play came in that caught the mood of the time, running 391 performances. Walter Greenwood's *Love On The Dole* (1935) dealt with life among unemployed Lancashire

The modern king of farce, Brian Rix, in Uproar In The House *(1967), a big hit. Elspet Gray (Mrs Rix) is on the right*

Michael Williams and Judi Dench scored another success as Mr and Mrs Pooter in Mr And Mrs Nobody *(1986), adapted from Grossmith's 'Diary Of A Nobody'*

cotton workers. It also introduced 23-year-old Wendy Hiller to the London stage, setting her off on a prestigious career. The theatre itself was unemployed from late 1939 to September 1941, when it reopened with a play entitled *Room V* by someone called Peter Wendy. Soon after, some ex-Aldwych farceurs – performers Robertson Hare and Alfred Drayton, and writers Vernon Sylvaine and Ben Travers – descended on the Garrick for much of the 40s. In between *Aren't Men Beasts* (1942), *She Follows Me About* (1943) and others, Michael Redgrave was excellent as the timid would-be murderer in *Uncle Harry* (1944), and Bea Lillie was hilarious in the revue *Better Late* (1946).

Debonair actor-singer-dancer Jack Buchanan took on the management of the theatre after the war, appearing in Lonsdale's *Canaries Sometimes Sing* (1947) with Coral Browne, and in Vernon Sylvaine's *As Long As They're Happy* (1953). Mainly comedies were presented under Buchanan's distinctive aegis, including Garson Kanin's *Born Yesterday* (1947) with Yolande Donlan, directed by Laurence Olivier; husband and wife Richard Attenborough and Sheila Sim in *To Dorothy A Son* (1951), and Robert Dhéry's French revue,

La Plume De Ma Tante (1955), which had mirth-filled audiences for three years. Then came the very English 1958 revue, *Living For Pleasure* starring Dora Bryan, Joan Littlewood's Theatre Workshop production of the Frank Norman-Lionel Bart musical *Fings Ain't Wot They Used To Be* (1960), and the Charles Dyer two-hander, *Rattle Of A Simple Man* (1962).

After a closure for redecoration between June 1965 and April 1966, farce re-established itself at the Garrick with the arrival of Brian Rix and his team, exiled from their home at the Whitehall by nude swimmers in *Pyjama Tops*. Such plays as *Stand By Your Bedouin, Uproar In The House, Let Sleeping Wives Lie, She's Done It Again* and *Don't Just Lie There, Say Something* happily occupied the Garrick from 1967 to 1971. Alastair Sim appeared in Pinero's *Dandy Dick* (1973), an older type of farce, transferred from the Chichester Festival Theatre. The genre gained a well-earned rest while Hollywood stalwart Broderick Crawford starred in *That Championship Season* (1974), a Joseph Papp production from New York. Alan Ayckbourn's *Absent Friends* (1975), and Ira Levin's ingenious thriller *Death Trap* (1978) took the stage before giving way to *No Sex Please, We're British* in 1982, adding another four years to its its 11-year run at the Strand. Bouncer, the theatre cat and also a shareholder, must have been delighted.

THE GLOBE

The Globe Theatre . . . a name redolent of Shakespeare's 'Wooden O' that stood on Bankside across the Thames until 1644. In fact, there was a second London theatre so named, built in 1868 off the Strand, and demolished after World War I. Neither had much in common with the noble domed structure that commands the corner of Rupert Street and Shaftesbury Avenue today.

Actually, Shakespeare has never been performed at the Globe, and when it was opened in December 1906 it was called the Hicks Theatre, after actor-manager Seymour Hicks for whom it was built. Thankfully, the name that suggests a theatre for out-of-towners, was changed in 1909. The architect was the omnipresent W. G. R. Sprague, who conceived it as the first of two similar companion theatres, the other being the Queen's on the Wardour Street corner of the block. The classical four-storey facade is decorated with four giant Ionic columns proclaiming the theatre's importance.

The auditorium, too, is in the grand, even somewhat pretentious style, with bold Corinthian columns framing the boxes. The Louis XVI ornamentation, and further columns, recur throughout the interior. A circular Regency staircase leads to an attractive oval gallery from which patrons can look down on the spacious foyer. Aside from some inevitable refurbishment and slight structural changes, the Globe is an extremely well-preserved Edwardian lady.

Seymour Hicks (knighted in 1935) appeared with his wife Ellaline Terriss in the opening production, *The Beauty Of Bath*. (It was a transfer from the Aldwych, the other theatre owned by Hicks, both in association with American impresario Charles Frohman.) Successful early hits at the Globe included *Brewster's Millions* (1907), with Gerald du Maurier superb in the title role

Five of the arches of the Globe's distinctive Twelve Arch bar, which looks down on the foyer

> 'If the past theatrical decade had to be
> represented by a single production, this is the
> one that many good judges would choose.'
>
> The Times on *The Importance of Being Earnest*, 1939

Ellaline Terriss (Mrs Seymour Hicks), one of the premier leading ladies of her day

brought the house down. Another funny lady, Jeanne de Casalis, created shock waves by appearing in pyjamas in *Potiphar's Wife* (1927).

Before H. M. Tennant took over the theatre in 1937, the French star Yvonne Arnaud sparkled in James Fagan's *The Improper Duchess* (1931), and in the revival of Fagan's *And So To Bed* (1932). Mlle Arnaud, a favourite with English audiences, had a theatre named after her in Guildford, Surrey in 1965, seven years after her death. In the first year of the Tennant regime, the lovely American actress Ruth Chatterton made her London debut in Maugham's *The Constant Wife*, and Owen Nares and Edith Evans starred in St John Ervine's *Robert's Wife*. In 1939, John Gielgud directed the classic production of *The Importance Of Being Earnest* with himself as John Worthing, Gwen Ffrangcon-Davies as Gwendolen, Peggy Ashcroft as Cecily and, essaying Lady Bracknell, for the first time, Edith Evans in her most popular and famous role. In later years, she began to hate imitations of her celebrated delivery of the line 'A handbag?' The play was not performed for

of the comedy subsequently filmed six times; George Grossmith and 'Gaiety Girl' Gertie Millar in the Oscar Strauss operetta, *A Waltz Dream* (1908); and Henry Ainley and Mrs Patrick Campbell in *His Borrowed Plumes* (1909) by Mrs George Cornwallis-West (the pen name of Lady Randolph Churchill, Winston's American mother.) Musical comedies and transfers kept the theatre full until and throughout World War I. In 1917, French music-hall star Gaby Deslys bid farewell to the stage in 'a musical affair' called *Suzette*.

The post-war decade saw the Globe under the management of actress Marie Löhr and her producer husband, Anthony Prinsep. Among their achievements were productions of Somerset Maugham's *Love In A Cottage* (1918) and *Our Betters* (1923), A. A. Milne's *The Truth About Blayds* (1921) and *Mr Pim Passes By* (1922), Frederick Lonsdale's *Aren't We All?* (1923) and Noel Coward's *Fallen Angels* (1925), with Tallulah Bankhead and Edna Best as 'those soused sluts'—as one critic called them. On the first night Tallulah, angry with Maugham for not letting her play Sadie Thompson, gazed out of the window and ad-libbed 'Rain!'. It

Gwen Ffrancgon-Davies (left), John Gielgud and Edith Evans in the famous 1939 production of The Importance Of Being Earnest

The award-winning production of Lorca's The House Of Bernada Alba *boasted magnificent sets and lighting by Ezio Frigerio*

another 10 years. It was a difficult act to follow.

At the beginning of World War II, Evans and Ashcroft, plus Alec Guinness, played in Clemence Dane's *Cousin Muriel* (1940). Plays reflecting the period were Robert Ardrey's anti-isolationist drama *Thunder Rock* (1940) with Michael Redgrave; Emlyn Williams' *Morning Star* (1941); Robert Sherwood's *The Petrified Forest* (1942), with Owen Nares in his last role before his death aged 55; and J. B. Priestley's *They Came To A City* (1943). But it was a comedy, Terence Rattigan's *While The Sun Shines* (1943), that cheered people up for the remainder of the war.

One of the most prestigious of post-war plays at the Globe was Christopher Fry's verse drama, *The Lady's Not For Burning* (1949). In the cast were Gielgud (who directed), Pamela Brown, Claire Bloom and a youthful Richard Burton. In the role of the drunken tinker was the great Shavian actor Esme Percy, then in his 60s. One night, during his big scene, his glass eye fell out. When a fellow actor stepped forward to pick it up, Percy said, 'Don't step on it, for God's sake. They're so expensive!' The following year Fry's *Ring Round The Moon*, a translation from Jean Anouilh, starred Paul

Scofield in the dual role of hero and villain.

Further memorable but contrasting productions that have kept the Globe spinning through the years brought Alec Guinness in *The Prisoner* (1954); John Gielgud (followed by Michael Wilding, then Robert Helpmann) in Noel Coward's *Nude With Violin* (1956), which ran a year despite luke-warm reviews; and two Graham Greene plays, *The Potting Shed* (1958) with the indefatigable Gielgud, and *The Complaisant Lover* (1959) with Ralph Richardson, Phyllis Calvert and Paul Scofield. The latter returned a year later in his most celebrated role as Sir Thomas More in Robert Bolt's *A Man For All Seasons*.

Comedies have been the staple fare since Scofield's dramatic *tour de force*. These have included Maggie Smith and Kenneth Williams in Peter Shaffer's *The Private Ear And The Public Eye* (1962), Donald Sinden in *There's A Girl In My Soup* (1966), Tom Courtenay in Alan Ayckbourn's ingenious trilogy, *The Norman Conquests* (1974), Vanessa Redgrave in Coward's *Design For Living* (1982), and a three-year run of Andrew Lloyd Webber's production of the schoolgirl romp, *Daisy Pulls It Off* (1983). In 1987, Glenda Jackson and Joan Plowright, leading a cast directed by Spain's Nuria Espert, appeared in Lorca's *The House Of Bernarda Alba*. Thus, drama was brought back into the Globe, a theatre worthy of its venerable name.

HAYMARKET, THE THEATRE ROYAL

There is no theatre that has more epitomized the experience of London playgoing for almost three centuries than the stately Haymarket. Only three London theatres are listed Grade 1 under the 1971 Act on the preservation of buildings of great architectural or historic importance, prohibiting rebuilding or demolition – the Haymarket, the Royal Opera House and Drury Lane. Of these three national monuments, the Haymarket is the only one where straight plays can be seen, the others being given over exclusively to musicals, opera and ballet. Its graceful John Nash portico, its opulent well-preserved interior, the premieres of plays by Oscar Wilde, seasons given by theatrical knights, and a string of glittering all-star productions, have made the Haymarket a byword for elegance and sophistication.

However, this most traditional of West End theatres had a rebellious youth. The first playhouse on the site, just adjoining the present structure, was built without licence or Patent in 1720 by a carpenter named John Potter, and called the Little Theatre in the Haymarket. Defying the monopoly which forbade the acting of 'legitimate' drama other than at Drury Lane or Covent Garden, Henry Fielding produced his satire on heroic drama, *Tom Thumb The Great* here in 1730. Further satires (by Fielding) attacking both political parties and caricaturing the Royal Family, resulted in the passing of the infamous Licensing Act of 1737, which reinforced the monopoly of the Patent theatres and led to the official agency under the Lord Chamberlain for the censoring of all plays. This ended Fielding's career as a dramatist and turned him towards writing novels.

When the actor Samuel Foote took over the theatre,

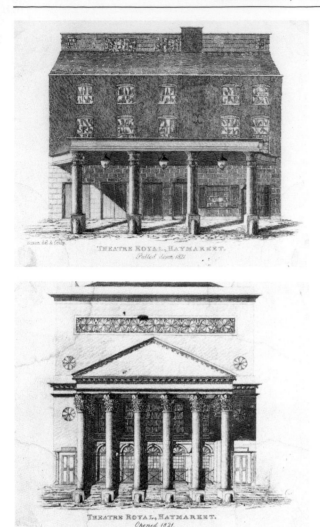

THEATRE ROYAL, HAYMARKET.
Pulled down 1821

THEATRE ROYAL, HAYMARKET.
Opened 1821.

*The old Haymarket (above) was demolished in
1821 and, in the same year, reconstructed as the
classical building familiar to us*

he successfully evaded the law by inviting his friends to
partake of cups of chocolate with him, and including
entertainment in the occasion. In 1766, Foote was
thrown during an attempt to ride the Duke of York's
unmanageable horse, a result of a practical joke. His
leg had to be amputated and the Duke, as compen-
sation, managed to obtain a licence for Foote to perform drama in the summer months when the other two
theatres were closed. Thus did London acquire a third
Theatre Royal. Foote sold the theatre to George Colman who carried it into a prosperous period, before
handing over to his son. Many plays by George Colman
the Elder and George Colman the Younger were performed during their time here, which was marked by
two violent incidents. In 1794, at a Royal Command

performance, the crowd was so great that 15 people
were trampled to death; then, in 1805, hundreds of
tailors gathered to protest at a revival of Foote's satire
The Tailors, which they saw as an offence to their craft.
The riot was quelled by troops.

The Little Theatre was closed for a while when Colman the Younger was imprisoned for debt. His
brother-in-law David Morris, who took control, left the
old building and built the present edifice a little to the
south of it. John Nash, one of the principal exponents
of 19th-century town planning, designed the theatre in
1821 so that its Corinthian portico could be seen from
St James Square. The theatre was described by a contemporary as 'in point of architectural beauty the most
elegant in London, but for the convenience of seeing
and hearing the worst contrived.' This apparently un-
pleasant auditorium was completely replaced in 1800
when Squire and Mary Bancroft took possession. The
changes made were radical. They created the first pic-
ture-frame stage by placing it entirely behind a proscenium arch. This was highlighted by a thick gold
painted border. They did away with the pit – the cheap
seats near the front – replacing them with the higher
priced orchestra stalls, which caused a first night riot.
Clearly, audiences were far more vociferous then.

In 1905, the interior was again replaced by that
which can still be admired today – a large house of 906
seats in a rich and elaborate Louis XVI style conceived
by C. Stanley Peach. Some improvements were made
in 1939, including a large and attractive lounge bar
which was constructed under the stalls. For a house
with such an imposing facade, it has a surprisingly
pokey entrance and cramped foyer where crowds
bunch up to get in. The theatre lacks, too, a decent
cooling system during the hot days of an English summer (not as rare an occurence as is generally believed.)
Nothing, however, has disturbed its slightly staid, old-
world charm.

The great actor-managers of the Haymarket in the
19th century were Benjamin Webster (1837-1853), J.
B. Buckstone (1853-1878) – his ghost is said to haunt
the theatre – and the Bancrofts (1800-1885). Under
these three regimes, the Haymarket became the fore-

*The gracious curved passage off the circle and,
inset, the ornate but elegant auditorium is
decorated in a handsome blue*

*'Mr Oscar Wilde's new play at the Haymarket
is a dangerous subject because he has the
property of making his critics dull.'*

George Bernard Shaw on *An Ideal Husband,* 1895

most playhouse in London. Famous actors that appeared here were Samuel Phelps in the 1830s as Shylock, Hamlet, Othello and Richard III; William Macready in *Money* (1840); Barry Sullivan as *Hamlet* (1853); the American Edwin Booth as Shylock (1861), and Edward Sothern repeating his New York triumph as Lord Dundreary in Tom Taylor's *Our American Cousin* (1861). His portrayal of the imbecile lord was so popular that the long side-whiskers he wore became known as 'dundrearies'. Sothern also created the title role in Tom Robertson's *David Garrick* (1864).

In 1887, the theatre passed into the hands of Herbert Beerbohm Tree. His most resounding success was

*Lily Langtry, mistress to the Prince of Wales,
made her debut at the Haymarket*

Trilby (1895) with himself as Svengali, the profits of which enabled him to build Her Majesty's just opposite. However, Tree's *Hamlet* of 1892 was a failure, giving rise to Oscar Wilde's comment, 'My dear Herbert, *good* is not the word.' But when the famous actor-manager produced and played Lord Illingworth in Wilde's *A Woman Of No Importance* (1893), Oscar commented, 'A charming fellow, and so clever: he models himself on me.' On the first night, Wilde arranged the house carefully, placing peeresses next to poets, dowagers beside young men, and his wife Constance in a box with Lord Alfred Douglas. There was a slight problem when the Prince of Wales refused to share the Royal Box with his mistress Lily Langtry. (She had made her debut at the Haymarket in 1881.) It was on the same night at the Haymarket that a blackmailer caught Wilde at the stage door and offered him, for ten pounds, the original of a love letter the playwright had addressed to him. 'Ten pounds!' cried Oscar. 'You have no appreciation of literature. If you had asked me for fifty pounds, I might have given it to you.' Another Wilde play, *An Ideal Husband,* had its premiere at the Haymarket.

After Tree planted himself at his new theatre in 1896, Frederick Harrison and Cyril Maude became the managers, sustaining and extending the tradition of fine plays, casts and settings. Maude gave outstanding performances in J. M. Barrie's *The Little Minister* (1897), Sheridan's *The Rivals* and *A School For Scandal* (both 1900), and George Colman the Elder's *The Clandestine Marriage* (1903). Other important productions until the death of Harrison in 1926 (Maude had left in 1905) were Maeterlinck's *The Blue Bird* (1910); the first licensed performance of Ibsen's *Ghosts* (1914), which caused a storm of protest; and Barrie's play of the supernatural, *Mary Rose* (1920).

The highlight of the war years was John Gielgud's repertory season of 1944-1945. The plays chosen were *Hamlet, A Midsummer Night's Dream,* Congreve's *Love For Love,* Webster's *The Duchess Of Malfi* and Somerset Maugham's *The Circle.* Gielgud featured in all five plays, while Peggy Ashcroft played Ophelia to his Hamlet and Titania to his Oberon. At the war's end, the sequence of civilized entertainments continued unabated, with the American actress Helen Hayes making her London debut as the mother in Tennessee Williams' *The Glass Menagerie* (1948); Ralph Richardson and Peggy Ashcroft in *The Heiress* (1949); Gielgud

Alan Bates (left) as the ill-fated Colonel Redl, with Michael Gough as Baron von Epp, the homosexual with a penchant for female dress, in the 1983 revival of John Osborne's A Patriot For Me

in N. C. Hunter's *A Day By The Sea* (1953); and Noel Coward and Margaret Leighton in Shaw's *The Apple Cart* (1954), considered by many to be the finest production of the play.

The Haymarket continued to skim the cream of England's acting establishment: Edith Evans and Peggy Ashcroft appeared in Enid Bagnold's *The Chalk Garden* (1956), and Ralph Richardson in *A School For Scandal* (1962), *The Rivals* (1966) and *The Merchant Of Venice* (1967); Alec Guinness was T. E. Lawrence in Terence Rattigan's *Ross* (1960), Trevor Howard starred in Anouilh's *The Waltz Of The Toreadors* (1974), and Maggie Smith triumphed in *The Way Of The World* (1984). In recent years Hollywood has come to the Haymarket in the shape of Claudette Colbert in *Aren't We All?*, Christopher Reeve in *The Aspern Papers* (both 1984), Lauren Bacall in *Sweet Bird Of Youth*, Liv Ullmann in Harold Pinter's *Old Times* (both 1985), and, most notably, Jack Lemmon – supreme in Jonathan Miller's quick-fire and powerful production of *Long Day's Journey Into Night* (1986), all of which brought the intoxicating glamour of one world into that of another – the Theatre Royal, Haymarket.

Rex Harrison and Diana Rigg headed the cast in a glittering production of Shaw's Heartbreak House (1983)

HER MAJESTY'S THEATRE

'My beautiful, beautiful theatre,' is what Herbert Beerbohm Tree always called Her Majesty's . . . and with some justification! Today, we can still see this grand old playhouse, more or less, as the great Victorian actor-manager saw it. However, until the early 1960s, its proud dome seemed much higher, for now it is dwarfed by the towering New Zealand House where the Carlton Hotel once stood. The theatre and the hotel were conceived by Charles Phipps in 1897 as an integral architectural unit, facing the Theatre Royal, Haymarket across the street. Of Phipps' theatre interior, still virtually intact, George Bernard Shaw wrote, 'He has had the good sense – a very rare quality in England where artistic matters are in question – to see that a theatre which is panelled, and mirrored, and mantelpieced like the first-class saloon of a Peninsula and Oriental liner or a Pullman drawing room car, is no place for *Julius Caesar*, or indeed for anything except tailor-made drama and farcical comedy.' In fact, it is luxurious but restrained, inspired by, but not attempting to equal, the classical forms of Ange-Jacques Gabriel's opera house at Versailles. It has similar triple tiers of boxes, framed by marble Corinthian columns with rich entablatures, decorated proscenium arch, and pretty 18th-century style paintings on the ceiling.

This consistently successful and attractive theatre has had three predecessors on the same site, and five different names. The first playhouse was built by the celebrated dramatist-architect Sir John Vanbrugh in 1705 and named the Queen's Theatre. It was destroyed by fire in 1789 and rebuilt as the King's Theatre in 1791. It became Her Majesty's in 1837 before being

Foyer and box office. Note the ceiling

The renowned Herbert Beerbohm-Tree in tragic mode

burnt to the ground 30 years later. It re-emerged from the ashes in 1877 as the Italian Opera House, and demolished in 1891 to give way to the present building. This edifice in the French Renaissance style with its open loggia, was called His Majesty's from 1902 to the accession of Elizabeth II in 1952. But under whatever name, it has made its mark on theatrical history.

It is highly appropriate that the present-day hit musical, Andrew Lloyd Webber's *The Phantom Of The Opera* (1986), should be housed in a theatre whose origins were mainly as an opera house. On this spot was performed Handel's first opera for England, *Rinaldo* (1711), followed by a number of others by the German master who became an English citizen in 1726. There were also English premieres here of Mozart's *La Clemenza Di Tito* (1806), *Cosi Fan Tutte*, *The Magic Flute* (both 1811), *The Marriage Of Figaro* (1812) and *Don Giovanni* (1817); Beethoven's sole opera *Fidelio* (1832); Gounod's *Faust* (1863); and Bizet's *Carmen* (1878). 'Swedish Nightingale' Jenny Lind made a sensational London debut in 1847 in *Norma* and other operas, and the first complete performance of Wagner's

Ring cycle was given at Her Majesty's in 1882. It only became a straight theatre in its fourth metamorphosis.

Under Beerbohm Tree, Her (His) Majesty's was one of the most distinguished playhouses in Europe. He carried on the Irving tradition of sumptuous, romantic productions of Shakespeare using many visual effects. The playwright Ben Travers described the realism of some of the productions: 'In *A Midsummer Night's Dream* he introduced live rabbits. In *Julius Caesar* . . . the actor who played Caesar was made to wear a bladder of ox blood under his toga so that when he was stabbed he bled profusely.' When Tree produced *Macbeth*, he recruited 50 real guardsmen for the battle scene. They used such force that during a dress rehearsal Tree cried, 'Stop. Never hit a backcloth when it's down.'

Between 1888 and 1914, Sir Herbert Beerbohm Tree (he was knighted in 1909) staged 18 of Shakespeare's plays, as well as melodramatic adaptations of *Oliver Twist* (1905), *David Copperfield* (1914), *Faust* (1908), and the first production of Shaw's *Pygmalion* (1914). The story goes that Tree, as Professor Higgins, kept fluffing his lines on the first night. When Shaw asked him to learn them better, Tree replied, 'But I do know my lines. I do!' – to which the playwright responded, 'Oh, I don't dispute that for a moment, Sir Herbert. I willingly concede that you do know your lines. But you certainly don't know *mine*.' Nevertheless, *Pygmalion* was Shaw's greatest commercial success, with Tree and Mrs Patrick Campbell's Eliza winning accolades.

In 1904, Tree instigated a drama school, which eventually became the Royal Academy of Dramatic Art, in rooms in the dome of the theatre. It was moved a year later to its present home in Gower Street. Sir Herbert's wife, Helen Maud Holt, shared his reign at Her Majesty's, and played in most of the productions. (In 1933, aged 70, Lady Tree returned to this theatre in *The Merry Wives Of Windsor*.) Her husband not only ran the theatre, acted and produced, but found time to have three daughters by his wife, and six children by his mistress Beatrice May Pinney-Reed, one of whom was the film director Carol Reed. A busy man indeed! This colourful character died in 1917 aged 64. On the corner of the theatre in Charles II Street, there is a bronze tablet commemorating his contribution to the reputation of Her Majesty's.

Tree always disliked long runs, referring to them as 'obstinate successes'. An 'obstinate success', if ever

'Tree took unofficial but characteristic action by making Her Majesty's serve some of the functions of a National theatre.'

George Rowell

there was one, came with Oscar Asche and Frederick Norton's 'Musical Tale of the East', *Chu Chin Chow*, which occupied the theatre from 1916 to 1921, the longest known run before *The Mousetrap*. It was, according to theatre writer Lynton Hudson, 'a cunning mixture of music, stage realism, and art pantomime, its constantly refurbished 'Folies-Bergerian' mannequin parade in frocks remarkable for their bizarre and gorgeous colour schemes.' It made a deep and lasting impression on the 12-year-old John Gielgud who saw it over 10 times. 'I was overwhelmed by the production, which fulfilled my most cherished pictorial enthusiasms,' he wrote. The oriental theme was continued in *Cairo* (1921), Somerset Maugham's *East Of Suez* (1922), and James Elroy Flecker's *Hassan* (1923) with incidental music by Frederic Delius.

C. B. Cochran, who produced Noel Coward's operetta, *Bitter Sweet* (1929), was told, 'It has no comedy, and the hero is killed at the end of the second act.' The

fashionable first night audience were, according to Coward, 'as responsive as so many cornflour blancmanges.' There was, however, much cheering at the end, mainly due to Cochran applauding and shouting, 'Author!', and Noel in the gods, crying, 'Cochran!' The show, containing the ravishing 'I'll See You Again' which was composed in a taxi during a long traffic jam, ran two years.

Further illustrious evenings at Her Majesty's offered J. B. Priestley's *The Good Companions* (1931) with John Gielgud as Inigo Jollifant; the legendary music hall comedian George Robey displaying his versatility as Falstaff in *Henry IV Part I* (1935); Ivor Novello and Vivien Leigh in Clemence Dane's version of *The Happy Hypocrite* (1936), originally a one-act play by Sir Herbert's half-brother Max Beerbohm; and J. M. Barrie's final play, *The Boy David* (1936), written for and per-

The cool and elegant bar lounge

Charlaine Woodard and Evan Bell in Ain't Misbehavin *(1979), the exuberant show based on the music and career of Fats Waller*

formed by Elisabeth Bergner. The war years saw mainly revivals of popular musical comedies before plays returned in 1947 with Peggy Ashcroft and Robert Morley in the latter's play, *Edward My Son.* Two Broadway hits, *The Tea House Of The August Moon* (1954) and *No Time For Sergeants* (1956) were among the few other plays to interrupt the string of musicals that has so often filled the 1261 seats of the theatre.

Alan Jay Lerner and Frederick Loewe's *Brigadoon* (1949) and *Paint Your Wagon* (1953) preceded Leonard Bernstein's landmark musical *West Side Story* (1958), which ran over two years. Also hailing from Broadway were *Bye Bye Birdie* (1961), *Fiddler On The Roof* (1967) starring Topol as Tevye the Milkman and running 2030 performances, *Company, Applause* (both 1972), *Bubbling Brown Sugar* (1980) and the return of *West Side Story* (1984). But now it is the home-grown *The Phantom Of The Opera* that continues to attract vast crowds to Her Majesty's.

The 'Hannibal' sequence from The Phantom Of The Opera

THE LYRIC, SHAFTESBURY AVENUE

The Lyric, the oldest of the six surviving theatres in Shaftesbury Avenue, blends into a block of buildings in the Renaissance style that stretches from Rupert Street to Great Windmill Street, with only its canopy and sign betraying its function as a theatre. However, the C. J. Phipps interior, redecorated extensively but tastefully in 1932 by Michel Rosenauer, dispenses the charm and atmosphere of a late Victorian playhouse. Giant Corinthian columns frame the boxes, attractive plasterwork decorates the large arch over the proscenium, and a handsome pale green and gold circular ceiling encloses the auditorium.

It was built for Henry Leslie, who made a fortune out of the comic opera *Dorothy* by B. C. Stephenson and Alfred Cellier at the Prince of Wales Theatre. Its 817th performance opened the Lyric in December 1888. *Doris*, by the same authors, followed in 1889. As befit-ting the theatre's name, operettas were the principal fare into the 1920s. Many of the early ones featured Marie Tempest, who only forsook singing for straight acting in 1899. W. S. Gilbert, who had quarrelled with Arthur Sullivan, delivered *The Mountebanks* (1892), music by Cellier, and *His Excellency* (1894), music by F. Osmond Carr.

The legitimate drama was strongly represented by the great Italian actress Eleanora Duse, making her debut in England in *La Dame Aux Camelias, Fedora* and *A Doll's House* in 1893. La Duse refused to wear make-up, and was able to blush or pale at will. Three years later, a play with a religious theme brought people to the Lyric who had never before entered a theatre. It was *The Sign Of The Cross* by Wilson Barrett, who himself played the Roman patrician converted to Christianity by his love for a Christian girl.

'It is fortunate that Phipps's interior (although altered) was not then completely devastated for the sake of fashion.'

John Earl *Curtains!!!*

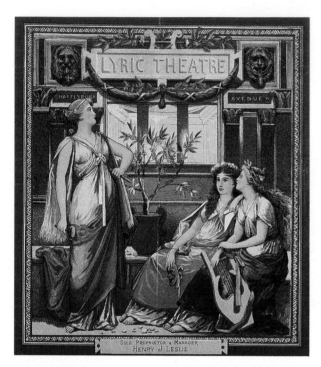

The programme cover for the opening hit, Dorothy, *in 1888*

Barrett claimed in private that he was a believer only as far as the box office was concerned, and continued to present plays of a similar nature, making him the forerunner of Cecil B. DeMille who filmed *The Sign Of The Cross* in 1932.

Not long after Duse appeared here, two of the greatest French actresses arrived in seasons of French plays – Réjane in 1897 and Sarah Bernhardt in 1898. Loie Fuller danced through nearly 200 performances of *Little Miss Nobody* (1898), and Evie Greene in *Florodoro* (1899) saw the theatre move profitably into the new century. In 1902 Forbes-Robertson, considered the greatest Hamlet of his time, repeated the role (he was to play it into his 60s), also taking on Othello and Kipling's *The Light That Failed*. His Desdemona in the former was Gertrude Elliott, whom he later married despite his affair with Mrs Patrick Campbell. Lewis Waller, known as 'the high priest of dignified tushery' appeared between 1906 and 1910 in *Othello, Monsieur Beaucaire, Robin Hood, Henry V* and *The Rivals*.

Musical entertainments such as Oscar Strauss' *The Chocolate Soldier* (1910), *The Girl In the Taxi* (1912), *Love And Laughter* (1913) and *Mam'selle Tralala* (1914), the latter three with Yvonne Arnaud, led up to the wartime hit, *Romance* (1915) starring Doris Keane. In 1919, she went on to play the female lead in *Romeo And Juliet* with the septuagenarian Ellen Terry as the Nurse. John Gielgud, Miss Terry's grand-nephew, recalled 'She could hardly remember a word, and Basil Sydney and Leon Quartermaine, who were playing Romeo and Mercutio respectively, whispered every line in her ear, and then she said the line herself and it sounded as if she had just thought of it.'

It was back to musical comedy with *Lilac Time* (1922) and *The Street Singer* (1924) before Tallulah Bankhead, the darling of the 'bright young things', drew the crowds in *The Gold Diggers* (1926), *Garden Of Eden* (1927), *Her Cardboard Lover* (1928) and *Let Us Be Gay* (1929). A dazzling sequence of stars and productions epitomizing the best in commercial theatre followed: Leslie Howard (just prior to his Hollywood debut) in *Berkeley Square* (1929); J. B. Priestley's ingenious *Dangerous Corner* (1932); Robert Sherwood's high comedy *Reunion In Vienna* with Alfred Lunt and Lynn Fontanne (later replaced by Noel Coward and Yvonne Printemps) in 1934, as well as Edna Ferber and George S. Kaufman's *Theatre Royal* (the English title of *Royal Family*), which starred Madge Titheradge, Marie Tempest and Laurence Olivier, directed by Coward. Olivier, playing a flamboyant character based on John Barrymore, slipped and fractured two ankle bones while jumping over a banister rail.

Olivier returned with his friend Ralph Richardson in Priestley's 'farcical tragedy', *Bees On The Boatdeck* (1936), which sank after four weeks. Vivien Leigh came to a matinee with Ivor Novello and sat prominently in a box, making Olivier upstage everyone in order to impress the woman he loved. Many years later (now his wife) Leigh herself held the stage at the Lyric in Coward's *South Sea Bubble* (1956). Critic Harold Hobson wrote, 'Vivien Leigh is the splendour of the production. Her performance shines like the stars, and is as troubling as the inconstant moon.' When she left the cast to have a baby (she subsequently miscarried), the play lost money.

Plays that had good runs without a dependence on big names were Rattigan's *The Winslow Boy* (1946),

John Moffitt, Helen Mirren and Joan Plowright in the hit comedy, The Bed Before Yesterday *(1975) by octogenarian writer Ben Travers*

Michael Williams (left), Judi Dench (Mrs Williams) and Richard Vernon in Hugh Whitemore's gripping play about the Kroeger spy case, Pack Of Lies *(1983)*

The Little Hut (1950), and the musicals *Grab Me A Gondola* (1956), *Irma La Douce* (1958), and *Robert And Elizabeth* (1964). However, stars such as the Lunts in *Amphitryon 38* – S.N. Behrman's adaptation of Giraudoux (in 1938) – and in Rattigan's *Love In Idleness* (1944); Deborah Kerr in *The Day After The Fair* (1972); Alec Guinness in *Habeas Corpus* (1973); Jessica Tandy and Hume Cronyn in *The Gin Game* (1979), and Glenda Jackson in *Summit Conference* (1982) did no harm to ticket sales. In the latter, a then unknown Gary Oldman had a role. Other future stars were Anthony Sher in *John, Paul, George, Ringo . . . And Bert* (1974), and Bob Hoskins in *Happy End* (1975). In contrast, 90-year-old Ben Travers, master of the Aldwych farce, provided a new hit play called *The Bed Before Yesterday* (1975) in which Joan Plowright (Lady Olivier) and Helen Mirren appeared.

Joe Orton's black comedy *Loot* (1984), which features a coffin on stage throughout, was playing to full houses when the lead actor, Leonard Rossiter, died of a heart attack during a performance. He had just made an exit, and collapsed in his dressing room. The show was held up for 10 minutes before his understudy took over. The Lyric recovered from the shock and was soon filled with Lerner and Loewe's melodies in *Gigi* (1985) and the laughter that greeted Alan Ayckbourn's *A Chorus Of Disapproval* (1986).

THE LYRIC, HAMMERSMITH

Once upon a time, an exquisite late Victorian playhouse was designed by Frank Matcham, the most renowned and prolific theatre architect of his day, for the London suburb of Hammersmith. It soon became prosperous and fashionable, despite its remote location, drawing crowds from the West End. The Lyric was, according to one expert, 'one of the best examples of *fin-de-siecle* theatre interiors in greater London – one designed by a master of the art of theatre building.' In 1972, despite public outrage, the theatre was razed to the ground to make room for property development. But the story has a happy ending. . .

Before the bulldozers could do their destructive work, the Greater London Council ordered that most of the plasterwork of the auditorium be preserved and stored. In 1974, the Hammersmith Council approved plans for a new theatre to be built as part of a modern development in King Street, not far from where the original Lyric stood. This was not to be just another theatre, but a complete reconstruction of Matcham's interior, using some of the original decor. The result is a curious but rewarding architectural experience.

The commonplace 1979 building which houses the theatre is located in a mundane suburban shopping centre. At the top of a stairway, one finds a roomy lounge, bar, self-service restaurant and large sunterrace or patio. Airy and relaxed, the venue provides a pleasant meeting place for people of the area by day, and for playgoers by night. Up another flight of stairs and one enters a time warp. There it is: the Lyric Opera House of 1895 with only slight alterations. The obtrusive pillars have been removed from the stalls, and the decorated ceiling has been replaced by an unattractive mesh behind which is stage lighting and venti-

A sketch of the period shows the original Frank Matcham exterior of what was then called the Lyric Opera House

'The Lyric at Hammersmith . . . was
uncomfortable and smelly, the dressing rooms
were wretched, but it had a unique atmosphere.'

Sir John Gielgud

*The Lyric's modern and spacious cafeteria is open
all day, a relaxing rendezvous, as is the
comfortable, airy foyer lounge, while the
reconstructed interior (right) is warm and stylish*

lation. The rococo ornamentation on the boxes and two circles has been retained. The traditional masks of Comedy and Tragedy adorn each side of the slightly enlarged proscenium arch.

Comedy and tragedy have played equal roles during the vicissitudes of the theatre's history. The first structure in Bradmore Grove, known as the Lyric Hall, opened in November 1888 with a French marionette show. Two years later, after reconstruction, it became the Lyric Opera House. In 1895, Matcham was commissioned to redesign the building completely. The tireless new manager, John M. East, produced over 400 shows, acted 120 roles, wrote the spectacular annual pantomimes, and invited stars like Lily Langtry and George Arliss to perform here. Alas, when East left in 1904, the theatre's fortunes plummeted, gaining it the sobriquet of the 'Blood and Flea Pit.' This decline was mainly due to a policy of presenting musty melodramas, and the rivalry of the new W. G. R. Sprague-designed King's Theatre (demolished in 1963) nearby.

In 1918, rescued by Nigel Playfair who redecorated it and changed its name to the Lyric Theatre, it became one of London's most popular and stimulating playhouses. A poem of the day went:

'No greater name than Nigel Playfair
Occurs in Thespian lore or myth;
'Twas he who first revealed to Mayfair
The whereabouts of Hammersmith.'

Many celebrated productions and performers lit up the Playfair years. His first success was John Drinkwater's chronicle play *Abraham Lincoln* (1919), which ran for a year. Athene Seyler and Herbert Marshall starred in *As You Like It* (1920) before the three-and-a-half years of *The Beggar's Opera* (1921), which Gielgud

found 'enchantingly pretty, too pretty perhaps, as the squalid satire of the play was lost. . . But how wonderfully he did it!' Gielgud himself appeared for Playfair here in *The Cherry Orchard* (1925), and as John Worthing in the 1930 Aubrey Beardsley-inspired black-and-white production of *The Importance Of Being Earnest*, opposite his aunt Mabel Terry-Lewis as Lady Bracknell. The later and most famous of all Lady Bracknells, Edith Evans, created a sensation as Millamant in Congreve's *The Way Of The World*. She also appeared in *The Beaux Stratagem* (1927) and *The Old Bachelor* (1931). Sir Nigel (he was knighted in 1928) had a penchant for the 18th century and revived Isaac Bickerstaff's comic operas *Lionel And Clarissa* (1925) and *Love In A Village* (1928) as authentically as he could. There is a Sickert portrait of Playfair as an over-age Tony Lumpkin in the present Stalls Foyer.

When Nigel Playfair left the Lyric in 1932, brightness left with him. In fact, it was literally dark for most of the period until after the war. Then, once again, playgoers made their way to Hammersmith for exciting productions. Two young actors returned from active service made an impact – Alec Guinness in his own adaptation of *The Brothers Karamazov* (1946) and Richard Burton in Christopher Fry's *The Boy With The Cart* (1950). John Gielgud directed the latter prior to his stunning 1952-1953 season of three plays. Gielgud directed Paul Scofield in *Richard II*, and *The Way Of The World* with himself as Mirabell, Pamela Brown as

Eleanor Bron in one of the Lyric's highly successful pantomimes, The Amusing Spectacle of Cinderella and Her Naughty Sisters

Millamant and Margaret Rutherford as Lady Wishfort. The third play was a rare revival of Thomas Otway's Restoration tragedy, *Venice Preserved*, directed by a young Peter Brook, and starring Scofield and Gielgud.

The Lyric continued to do diverse and interesting plays for the rest of the decade. Sir Donald Wolfit took on the arduous task of producing and starring in Henri de Montherlant's uncompromising *The Master Of Santiago* and *Malatesta* (both 1957). Challenging, too, were Harold Pinter's first play, *The Birthday Party* (1958), and Ibsen's early work, *Brand* (1959). Sandy Wilson's 'high camp' musical, *Valmouth* (1959), was delightfully frivolous and a smash-hit.

On 18 October, 1979, the Queen officially opened the newly resurrected Lyric. The première production, Shaw's *You Never Can Tell*, continued the great tradition of the theatre's previous life. The theatre, which is funded by the Arts Council, has a flexible studio theatre of 110 seats underneath the main auditorium, and offers lunchtime music, art exhibitions and children's matinees. Among its productions that have transferred to the West End – a sure sign of acclaim – have been Michael Frayn's *Make And Break* and *Noises Off, Charley's Aunt, Miss Julie, Kean* and *The Seagull*. In 1987, Maggie Smith starred in Cocteau's *The Infernal Machine* at the scene, or almost, of her first stage success, a revue called *Share My Lettuce*, produced thirty years previously.

The quintessentially English favourite, Charley's Aunt, *was a smash hit. Griff Rhys Jones (centre) starred, supported by Briony McRoberts (right) and Anita Dobson (left)*

THE MERMAID

In the area where Ben Jonson and his fellow playwrights caroused at the Mermaid Tavern, where stood James Burbage's Blackfriars Theatre for which Shakespeare wrote his later plays, and across the river from the site of the Elizabethan Globe Theatre, lies the Mermaid, the dream child of one man. It took the actor Bernard Miles, with the help of his wife, actress and sculptor Josephine Wilson, nine years to make the dream become a reality, and a theatre rise out of the rubble of a derelict wharf at Puddle Dock beside Blackfriars station.

It all started in 1950 when Miles decided to convert an old school hall at the back of his house in Acacia Road, St Johns Wood, into an Elizabethan-style theatre. The architect Ernst Freud turned it into an auditorium seating 200, with marble-painted columns, tapestries and white clouds painted on the ceiling. It opened in September 1951 with a performance of Purcell's *Dido And Aeneas* in which Kirsten Flagstad, Maggie Teyte and Thomas Hemsley sang. Some time before, Flagstad had been walking in the Miles' garden

when Bernard told her of his plans for the hall. 'I would love to come and sing in it,' said the great Norwegian dramatic soprano. And she did, on condition she had no salary but a daily bottle of beer. In the same season, Miles played Caliban in *The Tempest*, directed by Julius Gellner who was to become an associate director of the company. For the second season in 1952 *Macbeth*, in Elizabethan speech, with Miles and his wife in the leads, and Thomas Middleton's *A Trick To Catch The Old One* were added to the repertoire.

In 1953, as part of the Coronation celebrations, the Mermaid was reconstructed in the quadrangle of the Royal Exchange in the City of London, the first theatre in this district for nearly a century. The huge success of this three-month season led to the desire for a permanent theatre in the City. The site on which a disused warehouse stood was leased to Miles by the Council in 1956 for a token rent. Then began the years of 'endless thinking and rethinking, midnight oil, and candles

The spacious modern foyers

99

'I cannot believe that any new project on the London stage has ever had an audience more warmly on its side.'

J.C. Trewin, 1959

burnt at both ends', according to Miles. The architect, Elider L. W. Davies, shrewdly built the theatre in what was left of the warehouse, using the Doric columns for the entrance and the old dock walls as part of the structure. Attractive no, adventurous, quaint and atmospheric yes. The raked auditorium of 498 seats stretches down to an open stage, with the bare brick walls and exposed lights giving it a direct, simple and functional appearance. A handsome ship's bell is rung before each performance and at intervals.

The Mermaid had the great fortune to be launched with a hit in May 1959: Bernard Miles' adaptation of Henry Fielding's *Rape Upon Rape*, retitled *Lock Up Your Daughters*, with music by Laurie Johnson and lyrics by Lionel Bart, revived here in 1962 and 1969. At Christmas another Miles adaptation followed: *Treasure Island*, with himself as Long John Silver, a show which

Sheila Gish and Paul Hertzberg were Blanche Dubois and Stanley Kowalski in A Streetcar Named Desire *(1984) transferred from Greenwich*

became an annual event. The enterprising pattern of productions that emerged over the years was of a wide range of neglected masterpieces (*The Life Of Galileo*, 1960; *John Gabriel Borkman*, 1961; *The Bed Bug*, 1962; *Schweyk In The Second World War*, 1963; *John Bull's Other Island*, 1972); Elizabethan and Jacobean classics (*The Witch of Edmonton*, 1962; *The Shoemaker's Holiday*, 1964; Ian McKellen in *Edward II* and *Richard II*, 1969); and contemporary plays (*All In Good Time*, 1963; *Left Handed Liberty*, 1965; *Hadrian VII*, 1968; *Whose Life Is It Anyway?*, 1978; *Children Of A Lesser God*, 1981). Although a number of them transferred to the West End, the Mermaid has never gone for the soft commercial option, despite financial struggles, but rather tried to offer plays as off-the-beaten-track as its location.

Unfortunately, economic difficulties proved insurmountable for Sir Bernard Miles (knighted in 1969), forcing him to sell his beloved theatre to a big city firm and thus ending his involvement with it. In 1981, substantially the same Mermaid, but with an auditorium

enlarged by 100 seats and with more spacious foyers, was incorporated into an anonymous looking office block. But the anonymity disguises a lively theatre which is perfect as the Royal Shakespeare Company's second London home. *The Fair Maid Of The West*, and *Every Man In His Humour* (both 1987) put Ben Jonson *et al* back where they belong.

Elizabeth Quinn and Trevor Eve in Mark Medoff's
Children Of A Lesser God *(1985)*

THE NATIONAL THEATRE

On every first night at the National Theatre on the South Bank overlooking the Thames, a rocket is fired from the roof. It is known as 'Ralph's Rocket', because Sir Ralph Richardson suggested this celebratory ritual when the building first opened in 1976. There was much to celebrate, since it had taken over 70 years for the dream of a State-endowed theatre, especially designed for a permanent company, to become a reality.

Ever since David Garrick's day the need for such an institution had been discussed, but it was a book by critic William Archer and dramatist Harley Granville-Barker, *A National Theatre; Scheme And Estimates*, at the beginning of this century, that sparked off the debate in earnest. In 1913, the first of many proposed sites was acquired in Gower Street for a National Theatre. Another was in South Kensington where George Bernard Shaw 'turned the first sod.' On Friday, 13 June, 1951, Queen Elizabeth (now the Queen Mother) laid the foundation stone of the new building in front of the main entrance to the newly-constructed Royal Festival Hall. The stone has now been removed, and the site shifted a little further along the South Bank where construction began a mere 18 years later! In the meanwhile, the National Theatre Company was set up in 1962 under the directorship of Sir Laurence Olivier, and was housed 'temporarily' at the Old Vic Theatre for almost 13 years.

Finally, the long-awaited £20 million building, designed by Sir Denys Lasdun, took its place proudly beside the Royal Festival, Queen Elizabeth and Purcell Concert Halls, the Hayward Gallery and the National Film Theatre as part of an arts centre of international repute, unrivalled in London even by the impressive Barbican Centre inaugurated in 1982. It is certainly situated in one of the most attractive parts of the great capital, in the probable vicinity of the original Globe Theatre of Shakespeare's England. It looks out on a splendid reach of the Thames, curving past Somerset House towards St Paul's Cathedral, a scene not all that different from those painted by Turner and Canaletto.

This panoramic view of the noble and busy river can be appreciated from the many jutting terraces, both

The impressive Olivier auditorium (right)

'I think Lasdun's work is triumphant. He has divested concrete of its brutality. It is slender, delicate, and in beautiful geometric patterns. I think the theatre is a masterpiece.'

Peter Hall

open and closed, that form an integral part of the bold, unadorned, functional, concrete structure. The National Theatre itself is best seen by walking across Waterloo Bridge towards the lights that spell out the day's events, beckoning potential customers over the water. On entering the building, either from the river walk or from the bridge, one is welcomed by the roomy and relaxing foyers, a restaurant, seven bars, five buffets, and excellent bookshops. Before each performance, live music is played in the Ground Floor foyer. The building is open all day and the public is encouraged to use it as a social centre whether they see a play or not. In fact, more seating in the foyers and better lighting would be an improvement. Although a fairly large building, housing three theatres, it has an intimacy lacking at the Barbican, the home of the Royal Shakespeare Company – London's other large government-subsidized theatre.

Of the three auditoria, the largest and most radical is the Olivier, so called after the company's first artistic director and England's most famous actor. Sadly, Sir Laurence has never performed in the theatre that bears his name. Seating 1,160 people, it is fan-shaped with sharply raked seats in the stalls, slightly raised balconies on either side, and an upper circle all bearing down on the large apron stage, most suitable for epic theatre of which the opening production in October 1976 was a supreme example. It was a spectacular rendering of Christopher Marlowe's rarely-performed masterpiece, *Tamburlaine The Great* with Albert Finney powerful in the title role.

It was Finney as *Hamlet* (transferred from the Old Vic) who opened the 890-seat Lyttelton Theatre seven months previously. Named after the National's first chairman Oliver Lyttelton (Lord Chandos), it is of con-

A scene from Peter Hall's spectacularly dramatic staging of The Oresteia

Broadway came to the South Bank with Guys and Dolls. *The Salvation Army prayer meeting is here about to begin . . .*

ventional design with an adjustable proscenium stage, part of which can be lowered to form an orchestra pit. The seats are raked on two tiers facing the rather too-wide stage (especially for those seated on the side near the front), and is best suited to plays conceived in picture frame terms.

Completing the well-balanced trio of theatres is the Cottesloe, a small (approximately 400 seats), simple, flexible, rectangular room, which can be used for theatre in the round if necessary. (Lord Cottesloe was chairman of the South Bank Theatre Board.) There are two tiers of galleries on three sides, from which necks have sometimes to be craned to see the action. This provides an essential space for experimental or chamber theatre, or as a try-out venue for plays that might transfer to one of the two larger houses. It opened on Saturday 1 March, 1977, the first occasion on which all three theatres were in use simultaneously.

A decade later, the National Theatre has established itself as the powerhouse of London's theatrical life, despite much controversy and a continual struggle for sufficient funds to keep this vast enterprise afloat while maintaining a standard of excellence. The financial issue led to a running battle between Peter Hall, the artistic director since 1973, and the theatre's patron, The Arts Council, which has its purse-strings controlled by the government of the day. So serious did it

become, that Hall closed the Cottesloe for six months in 1985 'due to insufficient Arts Council subsidy.' It was subsequently re opened, thanks to a special grant from the now defunct Greater London Council. Richard Eyre, Hall's successor, has also to face the problem of surviving on a subsidy of only fifty-six-per-cent of the National's total running cost.

The aims of the National Theatre have been set out as the need to present 'a diversity of repertoire embracing classic, new and neglected plays from the whole of world drama; to present these plays to the very highest standards; to do experimental work, and work for children and young people; to give audiences a choice of at least six different productions at any one time; to take current productions regularly to the regions and abroad; to use fully the unique advantages of the building so that the public is continuously offered, in addition to plays, all kinds of other events.' On the whole, this manifesto has been admirably adhered to. As principal evidence of this, a look at what has been offered over a decade should suffice.

Among the many outstanding productions of classics, both ancient and modern, the National has

Angela Lansbury as Gertrude and Albert Finney as the Prince of Denmark in Hamlet, the first production at the Olivier (1976)

given Peter Hall's lucid and exciting production of *Coriolanus* (1984), starring Ian McKellen and using members of the audience as extras; Paul Scofield and Ben Kingsley in *Volpone* (1977); Peter Wood's sharp and glamorous stagings of *The Double Dealer* (1978) and *The Rivals* (1985); Shaw's *Major Barbara* (1982) and the complete four-and-a-half-hour *Man And Superman* (1981); Priestley's *When We Are Married* (1979), and Coward's *Blithe Spirit* (1976). American classics have been represented by O'Neill's *The Iceman Cometh* (1980); Arthur Miller's *Death Of A Salesman* (1979), *The American Clock* (1985), and *A View From The Bridge* featuring an exceptional performance from Michael Gambon, in 1987; and Richard Eyre's out-Broadway-ing Broadway production of *Guys And Dolls* (1982), which transferred to the West End for a commercial run. The NT's policy of commissioning established writers to translate and adapt foreign masterpieces has also paid off well. These have included versions of Musset's *Lorenzaccio* (1983) and Moliere's *Don Juan* (1981) by John Fowles; Chekhov's *Wild Honey* (1984) and Tolstoy's *Fruits Of Enlightenment* (1979) by Michael Frayn; Nestroy's *On The Razzle* (1981) and Schnitzler's *Undiscovered Country* (1979) by Tom Stoppard; Büchner's *Danton's Death* (1982) and Brecht's *The Life Of Galileo* (1980) by Howard Brenton; and the vigorously rhythmic and masked

Aeschylus trilogy, *The Oresteia* (1981) strikingly written by Tony Harrison.

Neglected plays given new life have included Granville-Barker's *The Madras House* (1977), Galsworthy's *Strife* (1978), Maugham's *For Services Rendered* (1979) and Kidd's *The Spanish Tragedy* (1984), the work that most influenced *Hamlet*. Some of the new plays presented were Alan Ayckbourn's *Bedroom Farce* (1977) and *A Chorus Of Disapproval* (1986), Harold Pinter's *Betrayal* (1978), Howard Brenton and David Hare's brutally funny exposé of Fleet Street, *Pravda* (1985) starring the brilliant Anthony Hopkins, and Peter Shaffer's universally acclaimed *Amadeus* (1979) which was first revealed at the Olivier with Paul Scofield as Salieri. If some people objected to the obscenities in the latter play, it was mild compared to the storm of protest over Howard Brenton's potent parable of colonialism, *The Romans In Britain* (1980). Its portrayal of a homosexual rape led to the director Michael Bogdanov being prosecuted by Britain's moral watchdog, Mrs Mary Whitehouse. The case was won by the National Theatre – not the last of their triumphs.

Peter Hall rehearses for the new 1987 Anthony Hopkins-Judi Dench Antony and Cleopatra. *The actors are, l to r, Michael Bryant (Enobarbus), Brian Spink (Demetrius) and Hopkins*

THE NEW LONDON

The aptly-named New London Theatre, built in 1973, lies in the heart of the old London area of Drury Lane. The very names of the streets surrounding it – Kean, Kemble, Macklin, Betterton, Garrick and Dryden – echo with theatrical history. On the site of the large glass structure, that could pass for a bank or office block, where tourists queue for the sixth year of *Cats*, once stood a public house called The Great Mogul, frequented by Nell Gwynn who lived nearby.

In the mid-19th century, the Mogul began to provide entertainment before becoming the renowned Middlesex Music Hall, where artistes such as Dan Leno and Marie Lloyd charmed Victorian audiences. Rebuilt by Frank Matcham in 1911, it continued as the New Middlesex Music Hall throughout the Great War, being the last of its kind to have a Chairman, the performer who introduced the acts from below the footlights. In 1919, it was taken over by George Grossmith and Edward Laurillard, redecorated, and renamed the Winter Garden. Leslie Henson (father of National Theatre player Nicky Henson) returned to the stage from the

army to star in the opening production, *Kissing Time*, a musical play by P. G. Wodehouse and Guy Bolton. He continued his association with the theatre in *A Night Out* (1920), an adaptation of Feydeau's farce *L'Hotel Du Libre Échange*, which re-emerged as *Hotel Paradiso* at the Winter Garden in 1956 starring Alec Guinness. Henson also appeared in *Sally* (1921) by Guy Bolton and Jerome Kern; *The Cabaret Girl* (1922) by Bolton, Wodehouse and Kern; and *Primrose* (1925) by Grossmith, Bolton and George Gershwin. Further musical comedies were *Tip Toes* (1926) by Fred Thompson, Bolton and Gershwin, and Sophie Tucker in Vivian Ellis' *Follow A Star* (1930); the Rudolf Friml operetta *The Vagabond King* (1927), and Gracie Fields in the revue *Walk This Way* (1932).

The lights were out at the Winter Garden for most of the 1930s, coming on again with *Peter Pan* (1942) in which Alastair Sim was Captain Hook for the first time, a role he was to play on and off for 26 years. The theatre

Cats – and more cats. It runs and runs. . . .

> *'The New London is a theatre of the future. It is a theatre that moves; stage, seats, lights – even the walls can be made to change their position.'*

Opening press release, 1973

was slightly damaged by a bomb shortly after Jack Buchanan and Elsie Randolph appeared in *It's Time To Dance* (1943), but it kept open just the same. Joan Temple's *No Room At The Inn* (1946), which dealt with the wartime evacuation of children, had a surprisingly good run at a theatre noted for much lighter subjects. When *Witness For The Prosecution* (1953) had been running a year, it was one of three Agatha Christie hits in the West End, *The Mousetrap* (at the Ambassadors) and *Spider's Web* (at the Savoy) being the others. Hollywood star Tyrone Power, who played in the film version of *Witness For The Prosecution*, was dashing as Dick Dudgeon in Shaw's *The Devil's Disciple* (1956). In 1959, the Winter Garden closed its doors forever.

The theatre stood as a hollow shell until 1965 when it was flattened to make room for a complex, incorporating shops, apartments, restaurants . . . and the New London theatre designed by Michael Percival. The

The New London escalators – more like an airport

result was a different environmental experience from the playhouses of yesteryear. Taking on many of the experiments of theatre architecture carried out on the Continent, it gets away from the concept of a fixed space. By having a third of the floor of the auditorium built on a revolve, and walls as movable panels, its shape can change from that of an amphitheatre to theatre in the round, from a studio to its utmost capacity of 907 seats, which can be raised or lowered.

The first performance here was a TV recording of Marlene Dietrich's one-woman show in November 1972, two months before the New London opened officially with Peter Ustinov's *The Unknown Soldier And His Wife*, an anti-war play featuring the author and his eldest daughter Tamara Ustinov. Also in 1973, the 25-year-old unknown Richard Gere (prior to his meteoric movie career) played Danny Zuko in the 50s nostalgia musical *Grease*. Other shows came and went until Andrew Lloyd Webber's music, Trevor Nunn's direction, Gillian Lynne's choreography and T. S. Eliot's minor verse came together to create *Cats* (1981). 'Now and Forever' is the slogan of that musical. It might not be an exaggeration.

Peter Ustinov (foreground) and Brian Bedford in The Unknown Soldier And His Wife, *which officially opened the theatre in January, 1973*

THE OLD VIC

There is no other theatre in London whose history is more imbued with the character of one person than is the venerable Old Vic. The spirit of this theatre was embodied by an irritating, God-intoxicated, 'undereducated', unmarried, bespectacled woman who hardly ever saw a play through. Yet Lilian Baylis probably exerted the most profound influence on the performing arts in Britain than anyone else this century . . . And she did it from her tiny office in the theatre she loved and seldom left, away from the mainstream of the West End. It is not too fanciful to argue that without her instinct, indefatigability and religious zeal, there would be no National Theatre, Royal Ballet or English National Opera, nor would English acting have acquired the international reputation it enjoys today.

Attributed with having prayed, 'Lord God, please send me a good actor, but send him cheap', Lilian Baylis was tight-fisted with money but generous with art. She didn't seem to care that patrons would catch their feet in the holes of the carpets, as long as there was quality on stage. Such was the prestige and joy of appearing here, that the greatest actors would accept miserably low salaries. She treated everyone the same; there were no stars in her heaven. Baylis used to cook bacon and sausages on a gas ring in the wings between, and sometimes during, performances. When Robert Atkins, one of the leading actors and producers in the company, advised her to go out and see what was happening in other theatres, Baylis replied, 'Not keen on plays, dear. Don't know what they're about.'

Tyrone Guthrie, soon to be a leading light as producer at the Old Vic, describes a visit he paid to the theatre in 1929 to see Gielgud's Shylock. 'The old house was shabby, even grubby. Rather rude and angry crones shoved a programme into your hands . . . But the house was packed, and the enthusiasm of the unspoilt, intelligent audience was infectious . . . the Old

Behind this handsome curtain have appeared all of England's most famous 20th-century actors

*'It smells and feels like a theatre, and is able
to transform a collection of human beings into
that curious, vibrant instrument for an actor
– an audience.'*

Sir John Gielgud

*The young Ralph Richardson was a delightful
Bottom in* A Midsummer Night's Dream *(1931)*

Vic audience, one felt, was composed of people who you could die to please, who wanted their horizons enlarged, who would come out to meet new ideas and new challenges . . . For the first time in my life I saw new social possibilities in the theatre.'

How did the Old Vic, as critic Ivor Brown wrote, 'become more truly Shakespearean in spirit than any regular professional theatre since the age of the poet himself?' The first hundred years of its existence gave little indication that it would ever become so. In 1816, it was proposed that a theatre be built in Lambeth on the South Bank of the Thames. It was to be named the Royal Coburg in honour of Prince Leopold and Princess Charlotte, who headed the list of subscribers. The architect was Rudolf Cabanel of Aachen, and the foundation stone and other materials came from the recently-demolished Savoy Palace at the foot of Waterloo Bridge, not far from the site. However, building progressed slowly due to lack of money until Joseph Glossop, stagestruck son of a wealthy Soho merchant,

put up the money and became manager when it eventually opened in May 1818.

Owing to the state of the roads and its unfashionable location, the Royal Coburg soon developed into the home of lurid melodramas for the local population. According to a contemporary writer, it was 'the very haunt and refuge of the melodramatic muse . . . where murder bares her red arm.' Nevertheless, none other than Edmund Kean acted here for a season in 1831, under the management of George Davidge who insisted that the Monday night working class audiences were succeeded in the middle of the week by 'the better classes, the play-going public generally.' In 1833, a redecoration and a change of name – it became officially the Royal Victoria, but known ever since as the Old Vic – did not disguise the fact that it was still a Blood Tub, the name given to a theatre staging crude melodramas at very cheap prices. In 1871, it was newly baptised the New Victoria Palace before closing down in 1880. In December of that year, the whole history of the disreputable building was altered.

Emma Cons, a doughty social reformer and first woman member of the London County Council, bought it, changed the entire interior, and the name to the Royal Victoria Hall and Coffee Tavern. With William Poel as manager, it was used for concerts, operas and scenes from Shakespeare. At the close of the 19th century, Miss Cons sent for her 24-year-old niece, then a music teacher in South Africa, to come and assist her. Lilian Baylis, whom Hugh Walpole called a 'first-class Cockney from South Africa', was born in London and went out to the colony with her family in her teens. Although she had had little previous connection with the theatre world, the management passed to her in 1912. Two years later, she began the bold experiment of presenting all of Shakespeare's plays in the First Folio at popular prices. This was achieved with the help of epoch-making producers like Harcourt Williams, Robert Atkins, Ben Greet and Tyrone Guthrie; and performers such as Sybil Thorndike, John Gielgud, Laurence Olivier, Ralph Richardson, Peggy Ashcroft, Edith Evans, Charles Laughton, Michael Redgrave, Flora Robson, Alec Guinness and James Mason. In 1923, the production of *Troilus And Cressida* completed the cycle of Shakespeare plays, making the Old Vic the first theatre in the world to achieve this. It must also be noted that opera and ballet performances

Laurence Olivier (seated) gave one of his many great performances in Strindberg's The Dance Of Death *(1967). Geraldine McEwan was his wife, Robert Lang her brother*

were being given at the same time until a second house was found at Sadler's Wells in 1931.

Lilian Baylis, 'The Magnificent Tyrant' according to James Agate, died in 1937. After a bomb severely damaged the building in 1941, the theatre was closed for the duration of the war. In November 1950, the Old Vic Company, after a glittering sojourn at the New Theatre (later renamed the Albery), returned home under the directorship of Michael Benthall. From 1953 to 1958, Benthall embarked on a 'Five Year Plan' to stage all 36 of Shakespeare's plays in the First Folio, beginning with Richard Burton as *Hamlet* and ending with John

A view of the foyer

The Tim Rice musical, Blondel, *reopened the newly refurbished theatre in 1983*

Gielgud, Edith Evans and Harry Andrews in *Henry VIII*. Both Burton and the aristocratic-looking John Neville were 'matinee idols' of this period. They alternated the parts of Iago and Othello in a 1956 production, and Neville broke new ground by playing Hamlet in a white shirt and jeans in 1958.

In 1963, this unofficial national theatre company was disbanded, and the Old Vic became the 'temporary' home (13 years) of the newly-formed National Theatre under Laurence Olivier, who directed the inaugural production of *Hamlet* starring Peter O'Toole and Michael Redgrave. If, as Voltaire states, 'History is nothing more than a tableau of misfortunes', then the history of the National Theatre at the Old Vic can only be described as a tableau of triumphs. With John Dexter and William Gaskill as associate directors, and Kenneth Tynan as literary manager, Olivier's own contribution was tremendous. In addition to his administrative duties, he played 13 roles including Astrov in *Uncle Vanya* (1963), in a cast that boasted Redgrave, Thorndike, Joan Plowright and Fay Compton, Solness in *The Master Builder* and an extraordinarily magnetic pitch-black *Othello*, both in 1964, and both with Maggie Smith. Among the new plays introduced here were Peter Shaffer's *The Royal Hunt Of The Sun* (1964) and *Equus* (1973), Tom Stoppard's *Rosencrantz And Guil-*denstern Are Dead (1966) and *Jumpers* (1974), John Arden's *Armstrong's Last Goodnight* (1964) and Trevor Griffiths' *The Party* (1973).

When the company, under Peter Hall, left for the new National Theatre in 1976, the Old Vic lost much of its allure, despite a smattering of good productions and a notoriously hammy Bryan Forbes-directed *Macbeth* (1980), starring Peter O'Toole, which crowds flocked to giggle at. However, in 1982, it was sold to Canadian entrepreneur 'Honest' Ed Mirvish who, in contrast to the penny-pinching Miss Baylis, spent over £2 million to restore the Old Vic to its former Victorian splendour. The stone and stucco classical facade and arched side wall in Waterloo Road were redecorated, and the auditorium with its lyre-shaped balconies was enlarged by 130 to 1078 newly-upholstered seats. With period wallpaper, fresh paint, roomy foyers and bars, and air conditioning, the Old Vic has been pleasantly rejuvenated. It opened with Tim Rice and Stephen Oliver's *Blondel* (1983), a musical followed by others such as *Seven Brides For Seven Brothers* (1983) and *The Boy Friend* (1984). These have done better than a somewhat curious choice of straight plays. But Shakespeare is continually drawn back into the theatre. After Michael Bogdanov's controversial productions of *Henry IV* (both parts) and *Henry V*, came the Royal Shakespeare Company's *Kiss Me Kate* (1987). In it, two characters sing 'Brush Up Your Shakespeare'. The Old Vic has always been the best place to do it.

THE PALACE

'The World's Greatest Artistes Have Passed And Will Pass Through These Doors' is engraved in stone above the stage door of the Palace. The claim is not an idle one, because 'artistes' of the calibre of Sarah Bernhardt, Marie Tempest, Anna Pavlova, Maurice Chevalier, Max Miller, Evelyn Laye, Cicely Courtneidge, Jack Hulbert, Ivor Novello, Jean-Louis Barrault, Laurence Olivier, Judi Dench and Natalia Makarova have played the Palace, one of London's most glorious monuments to musical theatre.

This High Victorian edifice was built, for Richard D'Oyly Carte in 1891, as the Royal English Opera House, to encourage the writing and production of home-grown operas. But to D'Oyly Carte's mortification, only the opening production, *Ivanhoe*, Arthur Sullivan's sole attempt at grand opera, was forthcoming from an English composer. He had to follow it up with André Messager's *The Basoche* from France. After its short run, and a Sarah Bernhardt season during which she played Sardou's *Cleopatra*, the impresario, who had brought Gilbert and Sullivan together, admitted defeat and sold the building to Augustus Harris in 1892. Harris immediately abandoned any idea of presenting operas here, and renamed the building the Palace Theatre of Varieties.

Although its days as an opera house were short-lived, the theatre retains the air and structure of such a place. In fact, Andrew Lloyd Webber and Tim Rice's 'rock opera' *Jesus Christ Superstar* (1972), and the musical *Les Misérables* (1985) have been perfectly at home here. Of the latter, Alain Boublil, who wrote the original text, says, 'this book (Victor Hugo's) is already a spoken opera . . .', and the composer Claude-Michel Schonberg writes, 'after the libretto was written . . . I decided, when faced with such an epic story, to employ a real operatic structure using a mixture of romantic

The foyer with its marble stairway

'The only theatre architecture of the last 60 years in London, or for that matter the provinces, which climbs into the regions of a work of art.'

John Betjeman, 1952

19th-century music with a contemporary mood – I am an opera fan so this exercise was very enjoyable for me.'

The building, occupying a whole block, partly in Shaftesbury Avenue, was designed by G. H. Holloway and decorated by T. E. Colcutt. The striking and unusual François I terra-cotta frontage (restored in 1987) facing Cambridge Circus has three bays filled with dozens of tiny arched windows, and at each corner domed towers rise above the parapet. Inside, a grand marble staircase leads up to the circle bar, also in marble, and down to the extremely attractive Palace Brasserie, looking as it might have done in the last century. The auditorium, seating 1450, has ornate gold mouldings and mirrors, and 'the deeply projecting galleries were unparalleled at that time by any theatre in Europe.' However, in 1959 John Betjeman expressed that 'Alas, the veined marbles which were so elegant and essential a part of its interior decoration have lately been defaced by a coat of plum coloured paint.' Fortunately, when Andrew Lloyd Webber's Really Useful Company took over the building in 1982, this paint was scraped off to reveal the marble and the Mexican onyx panels as being undamaged. The Palace is gradually being returned to its former glory.

Many of the glories of the music-hall performed here in variety bills for some years before revues became all the rage. American star Elsie Janis made a hit in *The Passing Show* (1914) in which Clara Beck sang 'I'll Make A Man Of You', one of the most famous recruiting songs of the Great War. In the sequel, *The Passing Show Of 1915*, Basil Hallam introduced the song 'Gilbert The Filbert' before he was killed at the front. Other revues of the period were *Bric-A-Brac* (1915) with Gertie Millar, *Vanity Fair* (1916), *Airs And Graces* (1917), and *Hullo, America!* (1918) in which Elsie Janis partnered Maurice Chevalier. A semi-Pierrot group

Restaurant and bar

called *The Co-Optimists*, of whom Stanley Holloway was a founding member, had a good run in 1924.

The tradition of musical comedy at the Palace began in earnest, or rather in frivolity, with Vincent Youmans' *No, No, Nanette* (1925), which ran 655 performances. Then *Princess Charming* (1926), *The Girl Friend* (1927), Jerome Kern's *The Cat And The Fiddle* (1932), *The Gay Divorce* (1933), Cole Porter's *Anything Goes* (1935) and Rodgers and Hart's *On Your Toes* (1937), which returned triumphantly to the same theatre 47 years later. In between this stream of musicals was a C. B. Cochran revue, *Streamline* (1934), in which Tilly Losch danced exotically, Gilbert and Sul-

Ballerina Natalia Makarova and award-winning Tim Flavin in the sparkling revival of On Your Toes

The people of Paris fight on the barricades in Les Miserables, *an international mega-hit*

livan were burlesqued, and Florence Desmond played 'The first British mother to fly over the North Pole with her baby.'

.From 1938 to 1945 the Palace was almost exclusively occupied by that madcap married couple Cicely Court-neidge and Jack Hulbert in *Under Your Hat* (1938), *Full Swing* (1942) and *Something In The Air* (1943). They made way for two operettas based on the works of Johann Strauss (*Gay Rosalinda*, 1945) and Edvard Grieg (*Song Of Norway*, 1946). During the long run of the latter, the theatre came under the management of Tom Arnold and Emile Littler. Over a year into the run of Ivor Novello's *King's Rhapsody* (1949), its composer-star collapsed and died aged 58.

Coincidentally, the great German playwright Bertolt Brecht, Novello's antithesis, died at the same age in 1956 in East Berlin while his Berliner Ensemble was paying a visit to the Palace on the invitation of impresario Peter Daubeny. Before they left for England, Brecht had told the Ensemble to remember that, as English audiences did not understand German, they were to play it 'quick, light and strong', to dispel any idea the English had that German drama was heavy. Daubeny also brought over other foreign troupes in the 1950s, including the Renaud-Barrault company and Jean Vilar's Théatre Nationale Populaire. The last in a short period of straight plays at the Palace was the transfer from the Royal Court of John Osborne's *The Entertainer* (1957) starring Laurence Olivier with his future wife, Joan Plowright (taking over from Dorothy Tutin), as his daughter. From then on it was musical entertainment all the way.

Imports from Broadway with British casts were Norman Wisdom in Frank Loesser's *Where's Charley?* (1958), two Rodgers and Hammerstein hits, *Flower Drum Song* (1960) and *The Sound Of Music* (1961), which ran six sentimental years, and Judi Dench in *Cabaret* (1967). Among the great big flops were *Two Cities* (1969), a musical derived from the novel *A Tale Of . . .* , and Betty Grable in *Belle Starr* (1970). Also showing lovely legs was drag artist Danny La Rue, wearing an array of gorgeous gowns for two years in the revue *At The Palace* (1970). Then came *Jesus Christ Superstar* (1972) which, according to Andrew Lloyd Webber, 'kept two then young British lads off the surrounding streets for nine years!' *On Your Toes* (1984) starred Russian ballerina Natalia Makarova, and was directed by 97-year-old George Abbott, before the Royal Shakespeare Company brought in *Les Misérables*. Nicknamed 'The Glums' by its director Trevor Nunn, it kept the Palace happy for many years.

THE PALLADIUM

Life Begins At Oxford Circus And Round About Regent Street, the title of a 1935 Crazy Gang show at the London Palladium, just about summed up what lovers of the music hall or variety (vaudeville in the USA) felt when approaching this enormous edifice of entertainment. For a variety act to have played the Palladium was equal in theatrical mythology to playing a two-a-day at Broadway's Palace Theatre. A list of all the famous stars who have appeared here would make up a 'Who's Who' of show business.

Until 1865 there stood on the spot a large mansion that belonged to the Dukes of Argyll and Marlborough (hence the names of the two streets that bound the Palladium). After it was demolished a firm of wine merchants built what was known as the Corinthian Bazaar. (The present safety curtain shows what it looked like.) From 1871 to 1887, the building was occupied by Charles Hengler's Circus and then, for some years, functioned as a 'Real Ice Skating Rink.' When a syndi-

cate led by the promoter Walter Gibbons (later knighted) acquired the site, it was decided that a music hall be built at a time when business was booming at such places as the Palace, the Hippodrome, and the Coliseum. The architect of the latter two theatres, Frank Matcham, built the Palladium facade by incorporating parts of the former circus building. With its six giant Corinthian columns on tall pedestals and statues at the centre and either side of the roof it could pass for a neo-Baroque temple, but for the canopy and the neon sign – one of the first to light up a theatre.

The vast, richly adorned and gilded auditorium with its two cantilevered balconies became familiar to millions on TV from the mid-1950s on with a weekly variety show broadcast called *Sunday Night At The London Palladium*. The M.C.'s over the years included Tommy Trinder, Norman Vaughan, Bruce Forsyth and Jimmy Tarbuck. The formula was revived for a new generation in 1987 with *Live From The Palladium* hos-

> *'The Palladium . . . attracts a large number of*
> *shoppers who patronise the performances*
> *before going home.'*
>
> Ronald Mayes, *The Romance of London Theatres*, 1930

Staircase to stalls from the foyer

revues such as *Whirl Of The Town* (1915), *The Palladium Minstrels* (1921), *Rockets* (1922), and *Whirl Of The World* (1923). The latter starred Nellie Wallace, Tommy Handley, later to come into his own on radio during World War II, and Nervo and Knox, who would return with the Crazy Gang in the 1930s. Revues alternating with the annual pantomime continued until 1928 when George Black reintroduced variety. Black, a theatre manager from the North of England, was the outstanding figure in music hall between the wars.

George Black's opening variety bill featured Gracie Fields, 'The Lancashire Lass making her first Palladium appearance', and Dick Henderson (father of comedian Dickie Henderson), alongside Ivor Novello and Phyllis Monkman in a one-act play entitled *The Gate Crasher*. In 1930, the Royal Variety Show, in aid of

ted by Tarbuck. Those who have had the pleasure of going to this theatre can testify to the surprising intimacy and atmosphere of the place. This People's Palace can claim, with a seating capacity of over 2,300, to be the largest live theatre in London, discounting only the Coliseum – slightly bigger but now an opera house. *The Era* of 1910 noted: 'Perhaps the most unique feature is the box-to-box telephone that has been installed. It will therefore be possible for the occupants of one box, recognising friends in another box, to enter into conversation with them.' Alas, this little convenience no longer exists, and waving and shouting must suffice from the paired boxes on each level in arched niches.

The Palladium opened on 26 December 1910 with a variety bill topped by Nellie Wallace, 'The Essence of Eccentricity', Ella Shields, and 'Mr Martin Harvey and his full company' in a one-act play called *Conspiracy*. Subsequent programmes mixed farce, ballet, opera, melodrama, song and comedy in two shows each evening and two matinees a week. Variety it was called and variety it was! All the most famous artistes of the music hall appeared here in the first few years: Albert Chevalier entertained with his Cockney coster songs like 'My Old Dutch', and George Robey was elected 'The Prime Minister Of Mirth.' One bill had Thomas Beecham (whose father was an investor in the company running the theatre) conducting operatic excerpts between the comic turns.

In 1912 Charles Gulliver took over the management from Walter Gibbons. Gulliver went in for spectacular

Yul Brynner played the King of Siam for the umpteenth successful time in The King And I *(1979). The governess was Virginia McKenna*

The Palladium hosted La Cage Aux Folles *(1986), a lavish, glitzy musical version of the hit film*

the Entertainment Artists' Benevolent Fund, was instigated at the Palladium, the theatre used more than any other for this annual event. It was also host to the Christmas presentation of J. M. Barrie's *Peter Pan* until 1938. The Peters were Jean Forbes-Hamilton (1930-1934 and 1938), Nova Pilbeam (1935), Elsa Lanchester (1936) and Anna Neagle (1937).

The Crazy Gang shows became another Palladium institution from 1932. The three pairs of comedians – Bud Flanagan and Chesney Allen, Charlie Naughton and Jimmy Gold, and Jimmy Nervo and Teddy Knox – brought back the low comedy tradition of 'the halls'. Their outrageous routines kept Londoners laughing until 1938 in lavish productions, always containing one number with the unprepossessing sextet in drag. Some titles were *Okay For Sound* (1936), *London Rhapsody* (1937) and *These Foolish Things* (1938).

The war years were filled with revues. *The Little Dog Laughed* (1940); *Best Bib And Tucker* (1942) starring Tommy Trinder, a favourite Buttons in the pantomime *Cinderella* here for some years; and Irving Berlin's *This Is The Army* (1942) in which the composer himself sang 'Oh, How I Hate To Get Up In The Morning.' On

George Black's death in 1946, Val Parnell took over the management and Moss Empires the ownership.

Apart from the Christmas pantos, often running well into the new year, Parnell introduced variety bills topped by big American stars from 1948. Jack Benny, Ethel Merman, Danny Kaye, Bob Hope, Bing Crosby, Fats Waller, Duke Ellington, Frank Sinatra, Tony Martin, Cyd Charisse, Phil Harris, Betty Garrett and Liberace were some of the names to appear on the Palladium's programmes. In 1964, Judy Garland, who had triumphed here in the 1950s, returned with her 18-year-old daughter Liza Minnelli. Judy dominated the show, and Liza's inexperience was cruelly exposed. But in 1973, now a star in her own right, Liza earned a standing ovation from the Palladium audience.

Although the Palladium kept variety alive long after it was said to be dead, there came a time when it had to ring down the curtain on what had been the mainstay of the theatre for most of its history. But *nil desperandum* . . . musicals were there to save the day. Yul Brynner played his most famous role in *The King And I* (1979) for English audiences, Michael Crawford risked his neck every night for two years in *Barnum* (1981), Tommy Steele attempted to follow in Gene Kelly's footwork in *Singin' In The Rain* (1983), and George Hearn and Denis Quilley camped it up in the opulent *La Cage Aux Folles* (1986) in the best Palladium tradition.

THE PHOENIX

Champagne corks and flashbulbs popped as London's glitterati poured in and around the Phoenix Theatre on its opening night, 24 September, 1930. It was not only a special evening because of the launching of Sidney Bernstein's new playhouse, but it was also that most fashionable of premieres – a 'Noel Coward First Night'. *Private Lives*, his brittle and now classic cocktail and dressing-gown comedy, was unveiled, starring the author and Gertrude Lawrence. The pair sparkled as ex-marrieds Elyot and Amanda on honeymoon with their dull spouses, played by the attractive Adrienne Allen and a devastatingly handsome 23-year-old named Laurence Olivier. Few theatres could have had a more glamorous beginning.

Noel wrote *Private Lives* as a vehicle for Gertie and himself in just four days, while recovering from 'flu in Shanghai. Of their first love scene on the balcony, Coward's biographer Cole Lesley wrote, 'Gertie and Noel looked so beautiful together, standing in the moonlight, that no one who saw them can ever forget; and they played the scene so magically, lightly, ten-derly, that one was for those fleeting moments brought near to tears by the underlying vulnerability, the evanescence, of their love.' The much-revived play got generally good reviews, but Ivor Brown in *Weekend* commented, 'Within a few years, the student of drama will be sitting in complete bewilderment before the text of *Private Lives* wondering what on earth these fellows in 1930 saw in so flimsy a trifle.' Despite full houses, the play closed after three months when it went to Broadway with Jill Esmond, whom Olivier had just married, replacing Adrienne Allen.

In 1936, Noel and Gertie returned to rescue the Phoenix from a bad patch with his programme of nine one-act plays under the title of *Tonight At 8.30*. In one of them, *Hands Across The Sea*, Coward took off Lord and Lady Mountbatten, but sent Lord Louis tickets for the first night. Mountbatten was not amused. 'It was a

The breakfast table scene from Coward's immortal Private Lives *in 1930. L to R: Adrienne Allen, Noel Coward, Gertrude Lawrence and Laurence Olivier*

'Private Lives *was decked in a glorious sheen
of success . . . and, in addition, was chosen
to open the Phoenix Theatre, a smart new
ornament to London's theatreland.'*

Cole Lesley

bare-faced parody of our lives . . . absolutely outrageous and certainly not worth six free tickets!' (Noel made amends with his 1942 war film, *In Which We Serve*.) On 12 September, 1952, Coward attended *Quadrille*, the Victorian comedy he had written for the Lunts, with gorgeous sets and costumes by Cecil Beaton. It was six days after he had heard that Gertie Lawrence had died of cancer of the liver. He found it difficult to sit through the first night in what Noel and Gertie used to refer to as 'our theatre'.

Seventeen years later, on 16 December, 1969, the owners of the Phoenix, Gerald and Veronica Flint-Shipman, helped organize a midnight matinee in honour of Coward's seventieth birthday. Noel entered

his box on the stroke of midnight, and friends on stage and in the audience, including Princess Margaret, rose to their feet to sing 'Happy Birthday.' A few days before, he had opened the swanky Noel Coward Bar in the foyer, the first thing that greets one on entering this pleasing theatre. A collection of paintings and photos associated with Noel line the walls. Coward died in 1973, the year that Vanessa Redgrave, Jeremy Brett and John Stride appeared here in a successful revival of *Design For Living*, the play Coward wrote for himself and the Lunts in the 1930s.

The atmosphere of the 1930s still permeates the

The magnificent mirrored foyer

En route to the plush Noel Coward bar

Phoenix with its Art Deco fittings, mirrored corridors and patterned ceilings conceived by the innovative Russian director and designer, Theodore Komisarjevsky (briefly Peggy Ashcroft's second husband.) In contrast to the modern, the classical is represented by the painted panels by Vladimir Polunin of reproductions of Tintoretto, Titian and Giorgione. The exterior of the Charing Cross Road entrance is also classical in style with its four, albeit rather jaundiced, columns. This entrance is awkwardly separated from the main entrance in Phoenix Street (next to a newly-built cinema) by an unappetizing apartment block.

The carefree early days of the theatre receded as the Munich crisis loomed. In 1938, Michel St Denis pro-

duced Bulgakov's *The White Guard* and Shakespeare's *Twelfth Night*, both with Michael Redgrave and Peggy Ashcroft, to acclaim. They were followed by a timely revival of Elmer Rice's *Judgement Day* (1939) about the Reichstag trial. The highlight of the war years was John Gielgud's production of *Love For Love* (1943) with himself as Valentine and Yvonne Arnaud as Mrs Frail. The critic W. A. Darlington noted that 'the crowds who flocked to see it were not impelled by a sudden realization of Congreve's excellence as a writer, but by his bawdiness.' It might be remembered that Arnold Bennett called Noel Coward 'the Congreve of our day.' Gielgud returned after the war as Leontes in *A Winter's Tale* (1951) and Benedick in *Much Ado About Nothing* (1952). During the former, Hazel Terry (Fred Terry's granddaughter) accidentally set herself alight and was doused by a fellow actor, the playwright John Whiting. Gielgud remarked before making his entrance, 'I hear cousin Hazel caught fire. The Terrys have always been combustible.'

Failing to catch fire here was Thornton Wilder's 'history of the world', *The Skin Of Our Teeth* (1945), starring Vivien Leigh and presented by her husband Laurence Olivier. This eminent theatrical couple appeared together in Terence Rattigan's Coronation year offering, a Ruritanian tale called *The Sleeping Prince* (1953) – filmed in 1957 as *The Prince And The Showgirl* with

Martin Shaw (left) brought Elvis Presley back to life in Are You Lonesome Tonight? *(1985). Simon Bowman (right) was young Elvis.*

Olivier and Marilyn Monroe. Rattigan, on much better form, had been here previously with his double bill of *The Browning Version* and *Harlequinade* with Eric Portman and Mary Ellis in the vastly contrasting pieces. Paul Scofield made a great impact in *Hamlet*, Graham Greene's *The Power And The Glory*, and T. S. Eliot's *The Family Reunion* from 1955 to 1956. There was a touch of Hollywood in the 1976 'Phoenix Theatre Season' of four plays – Rock Hudson and Juliet Prowse in *I Do I Do*, Glynis Johns and Louis Jourdan in *13, Rue De L'Amour*, Lee Remick in *Bus Stop* and Douglas Fairbanks Jr in *The Pleasure Of His Company*.

Although hits at the Phoenix in the 1980s have not been too frequent, long runs over the years have included Cicely Courtneidge in *Under The Counter* (1945, for two years), Lesley Storm's *Roar Like A Dove* (1957, for three years), *Canterbury Tales* (1968, for five years) and Tom Stoppard's *Night And Day* (1978 for two years). In 1985, Martin Shaw successfully burst in as Elvis Presley in the bio-musical *Are You Lonesome Tonight?* – a far cry from Noel and Gertie singing the wistful 'Someday I'll Find You' at the elegant opening all those years ago.

THE PICCADILLY

In the souvenir programme that accompanied the opening of the Piccadilly Theatre in April 1928, it was stated that if all the bricks used in its construction were placed end to end in a straight line, they would have stretched from London to Paris. This was another way of saying that the theatre was a huge construction, one of the largest built in London in the 20th century. Designed by Bertie Crewe and Edward A. Stone for the impresario Edward Laurillard, its 1,400 seat auditorium aimed more for space and comfort than for atmosphere and intimacy. There were elongated bars on the three levels, and beautifully equipped Ladies Salons with rows of dressing tables and mirrors to assist any necessary facial refurbishment. The fittings and decoration in green and gold were carried out in the modernist (Art Deco) style by Marc-Henri and Laverdet, as the French designers Marc-Henri Levy and Gaston Laverdet were known. The attractive four-storey Portland stone facade curves gracefully round the corner on which the theatre stands, vaguely influenced by John Nash's classical frontages in Regent Street only a few yards away.

Evelyn Laye, 'easily the most popular musical comedy actress of our time', starred in the first production here, Jerome Kern's *Blue Eyes*, which ran four months before transferring. For the next year, the theatre was used by Warner Bros. for the showing of 'talkies', starting with Al Jolson's second film, *The Singing Fool*. Live theatre returned in November 1929 with a revival of *The Student Prince*. A very mixed batch of productions ensued, failing to give the Piccadilly any distinctive personality or policy, a situation that continues to the present day.

Up to the outbreak of war, the theatre played host to Cicely Courtneidge in a revue entitled *Folly To Be Wise* (1931), Robert Donat and Ernest Thesiger in James

The stage, and the auditorium which seats 1150

'In May 1973 success arrived at last with Gypsy starring Angela Lansbury'

Mander & Mitchenson

Bridie's *A Sleeping Clergyman* (1933), and Gwen Ffrangcon-Davies in *The Barretts Of Wimpole Street* (1935). The character of the Piccadilly was epitomized in a *mélange* called *Choose Your Time*. It consisted of a continuous programme of variety turns, a swing band, newsreels, cartoons and *Talk Of The Devil*, a short play with Yvonne Arnaud and John Mills.

In 1941, Noel Coward's *Blithe Spirit* had its premiere here. The hugely popular 'supernatural' comedy, starring Cecil Parker, Fay Compton, Kay Hammond, and Margaret Rutherford as the eccentric clairvoyant Madame Arcati, soon transferred to the St James' (since demolished) and the Duchess to complete an amazing 1997 performances. After touring with *Macbeth* (1942), John Gielgud brought it in to the Piccadilly for a few 'exhausting and not very successful'

months. (Incidentally, Ernest Thesiger played the First Witch.) The bad luck said to attend 'the Scottish play' lingered on into 1943, when the theatre was damaged by a flying bomb attack.

In 1945, the year of its reopening, Noel Coward's revue *Sigh No More* was seen. It featured Joyce Grenfell, Cyril Ritchard, and Noel's close friend Graham Payn for whom he wrote the song 'Matelot'. Edith Evans and Godfrey Tearle tackled *Anthony And Cleopatra* (1946), and John Van Druten's *The Voice Of The Turtle* (1947) was coldly received. Short runs and transfers occupied the Piccadilly until the interior was completely redecorated in a streamlined rather anonymous manner in 1955, the red plush seating being reduced to 1150.

In the five years leading up to the acquisition of the theatre by Donald Albery (against stiff competition

Arthur Hill and Uta Hagen as the married sparring partners in Who's Afraid Of Virginia Woolf? *(1964)*

from Bernard Delfont) four comedies stood out. Peter Ustinov in his own *Romanoff And Juliet* (1956); Richard Attenborough, John Clements, Kay Hammond and Constance Cummings in *The Rape Of The Belt* (1957) by Cummings' husband Benn W. Levy; *Hook, Line And Sinker* (1958) with Joan Plowright and Robert Morley; and the real-life married couple Clements and Hammond in *The Marriage Go Round* (1959).

However, it was American drama and musicals that gave the Piccadilly some prestige in the 60s and 70s. The original Broadway leads, Uta Hagen and Arthur Hill, in Edward Albee's scabrous *Who's Afraid Of Virginia Woolf?* (1964), and Richard Kiley in *Man Of La Mancha* (1969) brought authority to those productions, as did Angela Lansbury in *Gypsy* (1973), Claire Bloom in *A Streetcar Named Desire* (1974), and Henry Fonda in his solo performance as *Clarence Darrow* (1975). The Royal Shakespeare Company brought some of their productions here while waiting for the Barbican to open, including the hit, *Educating Rita* (1980), with Julie Walters. In 1982, the auditorium was transformed into a nightclub during the run of a magic show called *Y*, and the 'Prompt Corner' Bar and Disco added. The spectacular British musical *Mutiny* (1985), despite bad notices, managed to keep afloat for over a year. And the Piccadilly sails on. . .

Julie Walters, who went on to star in the film of Educating Rita, *with Mark Kingston in the 1980 RSC production at the Piccadilly*

THE PRINCE EDWARD

For the last nine years crowds have been making their way past sex shops, pubs and restaurants in the lively, cosmopolitan, rather sleazy area of Soho to a brown-brick building in the shape of an Italian *palazzo* on the corner of Greek and Old Compton Streets. Behind the sturdy square facade, decorated unostentatiously with four pillars, are the salubrious surroundings of the spacious circular lobby lit by a large chandelier, and the pink and red plush cinema-style auditorium. In fact, the Prince Edward simply reeks of the sleek satisfaction that comes from having had the smash-hit musical *Evita* (1978) here for eight fat years, followed by another musical success, *Chess* (1986), booking over a year ahead. But this money-making milieu did

not come about overnight. *Chess* may be packing them in now, but the theatre itself has had an extremely chequered career.

This chameleon of a structure has been variously a theatre, a cabaret-restaurant, a servicemen's club, a trade show cinema, and the home of Cinerama. It has staged musicals, revues, variety, pantomimes, floor shows and ballet. It has also had three names. On the spot where it was built in 1930, stood a vast draper's shop known as The Emporium. Although Royalty and other nobs patronised it, it began losing trade in the 1920s and was demolished. The building that arose on the site was the first of four new theatres opened in London in 1930. All of them – the Cambridge, the

The 'picture palace' foyer

Phoenix, the Whitehall and the Prince Edward – went for the latest in interior decoration, much of which was what we now call Art Deco. The interior designers, Marc-Henri and Laverdet, went for rectilinear patterns and René Lalique amber glass to frame the proscenium arch. Alas, this has vanished now.

Coincidentally, the theatre that finally came into its own with *Evita*, kicked off with another Latin American senorita. The popular Broadway operetta of the 1920s, *Rio Rita*, was chosen as the opening production. Unfortunately, the show that Ziegfeld presented so successfully in the USA, failed to take off in the U.K. Other short-lived musical comedies followed with only *Nippy* (1930), starring Binnie Hale, managing to get beyond a hundred performances. Not even the wonderful black American cabaret artiste, Josephine Baker, the toast of Paris, could fill the theatre in 1933. Non-stop revue from 2 p.m. to midnight was tried until the management, admitting defeat, leased the building for the use of trade film shows.

However, thanks to a syndicate which included the theatre's architect, E. A. Stone, it opened in April 1936 as the London Casino, having been converted skilfully,

The auditorium, showing its 30s-style boxes

> '*To* Evita *this evening at the Prince Edward
> . . . It's the cult of kitsch again, inert,
> calculating, camp and morally questionable. I
> felt out of step with popular taste . . .*'

Peter Hall (*Diaries*)

and at a cost of £25,000, into a cabaret-restaurant. A dance floor and stairways from the stalls to the dress circle were constructed. Business boomed as people flocked to dine, dance and watch spectacular stage shows such as *Folies Parisiennes*. But the party was over in 1940, when the London Casino had to close down during wartime and became the Queensbury All-Services Club.

Tom Arnold and Emile Littler changed it back into a theatre, again called the London Casino. *Pick-Up-Girl* (1946) retained the air of naughtiness, dispelled by a revival of Ivor Novello's operetta *The Dancing Years* (1947). A mish-mash of variety, ballet, pantomimes and musicals continued for the next few years. These included the French-style 'Les Girls' show, *Latin Quarter* (1949), Cicely Courtneidge in a revue called *Over*

Elaine Page and Joss Ackland were the notorious Perons in Evita

The Moon (1953), and *Wish You Were Here*, a musical set in a holiday camp and the last stage production before the arrival of *Cinerama Holiday* in 1954. A flashing sign proclaimed the newest big-screen fad, and *How The West Was Won* (1962) as well as *2001: A Space Odyssey* (1968) were shown here.

In 1974, the Delfont Organisation took over the ownership, redecorated the building, and used it as a cinema but for the occasional annual pantomime. Reverting to its original name, the Prince Edward opened its doors to *Evita* in 1978, and it was a case of 'Don't cry for me anymore.' The Andrew Lloyd Webber-Tim Rice politico-rock musical, with a sensational Elaine Page, an unknown in the title role, put British musicals firmly on the map. Then, from the unlikeliest of subjects, Tim Rice and members of the pop group Abba, aided by RSC director Trevor Nunn and New York designer Theoni V. Aldredge, fashioned *Chess* into another block-busting hit for the Prince Edward.

THE PRINCE OF WALES

If a vote were to be taken on the best location for a theatre in the West End, the key position on the corner of Coventry and Oxendon Streets where stands the Prince of Wales, would surely win. The crowds of revellers, streaming between Piccadilly Circus and Leicester Square cannot fail to see the dominating once-white artificial-stone building with its huge sign and belfry-like tower. Its favourable position has certainly helped to fill its 1,139 seats since it was built in 1937.

The first theatre on the site, called simply the Prince's, was designed by C. J. Phipps as an exotic affair with a Moorish style foyer and smoking room. It opened in January 1884 with Beerbohm Tree in W. S. Gilbert's 'Fairy Comedy', *The Palace of Truth*. Tree also appeared in a free adaptation of Ibsen's *A Doll's House* called *Breaking A Butterfly*, and in Charles Hawtrey's farce *The Private Secretary*, both in the year of the theatre's inauguration. In 1885, Tree played Joseph Surface to Lily Langtry's Lady Teazle in *The School For Scandal*. 'The Jersey Lily' returned for a season of plays in 1886, the year the Prince's, coincidentally, changed its title to the Prince Of Wales, named after the actress' intimate friend. The success of the comic opera *Dorothy* (1887), which ran a year, led the producer, Henry J. Leslie, to build the Lyric, Shaftesbury Avenue from its profits. The appearance of the 'wordless play' *L'Enfant Prodigue* from France, with mimes Jane May and Zanfretta, led to the establishment of the first Pierrot troupe in England.

According to a definition, musical comedy is 'a popular type of light entertainment which derives from a fusion of burlesque and light opera.' Thus George Edwardes' *In Town* (1892) has the distinction of being considered the first true musical comedy. Another example of the new genre as presented by Edwardes was *The Gaiety Girl* (1893). Apart from musical comedy, Mrs Patrick Campbell and Forbes-Robertson performed in Maurice Maeterlinck's symbolist drama *Pelléas And Mélisande* with incidental music by Fauré. Marie Tempest, having deserted Edwardes and musical

The large, poster-decorated bar

*'A curious medley of song, dance and nonsense
. . . and the very vaguest attempt at satirising
the modern masher.'*

Sunday Times on *In Town*, 1892

*Linda Baron was the mature Belle Poitrine in the
musical version of Patrick Dennis' Little Me (1984)*

comedy, played in three adaptations from novels: *English Nell* from Anthony Hope, *Peg Woffington*, from Charles Read, and *Becky Sharp* from Thackeray's *Vanity Fair*, all between 1900-1901. Edwardes' musical comedies returned from 1903-1910; 'Man-about-town' Charles Hawtrey appeared in comedies from 1912-1918, and Bea Lillie, Gertie Lawrence, Jack Buchanan and Jessie Matthews featured in André Charlot revues from 1918-1926. Things deteriorated somewhat in the 1930s as the Prince of Wales resorted to Non-Stop Revue which was only halted by the demolition of the theatre in 1937.

The foundation stone of the new house, which opened in October 1937, was laid by Gracie Fields. The architect, Robert Cromie, conceived a large two-tier theatre with the circle front within 21 feet of the orchestra. The auditorium has a slightly cavernous feel, but the enormous stalls bar has room for an impressive archive of playbills of the many shows that have played here. Among them were the successes under the management of George Black in the 1940s. He introduced comedian Sid Field to London audiences in *Strike A New Note* in 1943. Field also shone in *Strike It Again* (1944), *Piccadilly Hayride* (1946), and finally *Harvey* (1949), the Mary Chase Broadway hit about an amiable drunk with an imaginary giant white rabbit as a friend. Sadly, Field died at the age of 46 during its long run. *Harvey* returned to the Prince of Wales in 1975, when Hollywood star James Stewart repeated his New York

*The famous legs of Juliet Prowse were used to good
effect in* Sweet Charity *(1967), a superior musical
based on Fellini's* Nights Of Cabiria

stage role of Elwood P. Dowd, the drunk, which he had also played on the screen in 1950. Another legendary movie star, Mae West, appeared here briefly in *Diamond Lil* in 1948.

For much of the 1950s the theatre was given over to traditional variety shows, featuring Benny Hill, Frankie Howerd and Norman Wisdom, until *The World Of Suzie Wong* (1959) – called by critic Kenneth Tynan 'The World Of Woozey Song' – arrived for a run of almost three years. American comedies and musicals were to be the principal fare from then on. Neil Simon's first play, *Come Blow Your Horn* (1962) had a good run, but it was Barbra Streisand's dynamic presence in *Funny Girl* (1966) that had the queues collecting in Coventry Street. Streisand was some months pregnant at the time (by her then husband Elliot Gould), so the show's run was limited. Other imports were the splendid *Sweet Charity* (1967) starring Juliet Prowse, *Promises Promises* (1969), *Same Time Next Year* (1976), *I Love My Wife* (1977), and *Little Me* (1984). Homegrown productions included *The Good Old Bad Old Days* (1972), directed, starring and written (with Leslie Bricusse) by Anthony Newley; *Underneath The Arches* (1982), a tribute to Flanagan and Allen; and *'Allo 'Allo* (1986), a comedy derived from TV about the French resistance, which vast sections of the population found irresistible.

THE QUEENS

In the heart of 'theatreland', on the corner of Shaftesbury Avenue and Wardour Street, stands a modern glass-fronted, red-brick, five-storey building that houses the Queen's Theatre. If one wonders, while contemplating the pleasing but unexceptional 1959 facade, what the 1907 playhouse once looked like, then one has only to walk a few yards to the Globe Theatre on the Rupert Street corner of the block. They were designed by W. G. R. Sprague as near-identical twin theatres. Today, they could not be more dissimilar.

Some people might agree with John Earl's views on the exterior of the Queen's (see the quote), but few could fail to be charmed by the red, white and gold auditorium, with its domed ceiling and Louis XVI-style plaster ornamentation, which creates an elegant Edwardian atmosphere. The reason why the Globe exterior remains little altered from its inception in 1906, while its twin resides in a modern shell, is that a German bomb fell on the unfortunate Queen's in Sep-

tember 1940, destroying much of the facade and the back of the stalls. It is ironic that the first London theatre casualty of the war should be a theatre which has had fewer theatrical bombs than most.

However, the Queen's took some years to make its reputation. The opening production – *The Sugar Bowl* (1907), a comedy with Edmund Gwenn – was a flop, allowing Shaw's *The Devil's Disciple* to transfer from the Savoy. H. B. Irving took over the management in 1909, appearing in a number of his famous father Henry's famous barnstorming parts, such as *The Bells*, *Louis XI* and *The Lyons Mail*. But in 1913, blood and thunder gave way to 'Tango Teas' for which the stalls were transformed into a dance floor with tables placed around it so that the patrons could partake in tea, and dance the fashionable tango, all for half-a-crown.

When the strains of the tango had died away, the

The ceiling in detail

*'No doubt in 1957 the restoration of the facade
. . . was seen as exciting and new. Now it looks
outdated, un-theatrelike, and even heartless.'*

John Earl in *Curtains!!!*

sound of applause returned to the building for the American Jewish comedy *Potash And Perlmutter* (1914), and its sequel *Potash And Perlmutter In Society* (1916). In the 20s, the theatre welcomed Alfred Savoir's *Bluebeard's Eighth Wife* (1922), Fred and Adele Astaire in *Stop Flirting* (1923), Owen Nares and Fay Compton in J. M. Barrie's *The Little Minister* (1924), and Edmund Gwenn and Yvonne Arnaud as Mr and Mrs Pepys in *And So To Bed* (1926).

From 1929, the stage of the Queen's held a dazzling array of stars and stars-to-be that must elicit the inevitable phrase 'the good old days.' Cedric Hardwicke (knighted in 1934) appeared as Magnus in *The Apple Cart* (1929) and Mr Barrett in *The Barretts Of Wimpole Street* (1930) with Gwen Ffrangcon-Davies as Elizabeth; Edith Evans was in *The Apple Cart, Heartbreak House* (1932) and *Once In A Lifetime* (1933); and Marie Tempest, Sybil Thorndike, Margaret Rutherford, Ursula Jeans and Rex Harrison were assembled for Robert Morley's first play, *Short Story* (1935). But it was John Gielgud's presence that dominated the Queen's from 1937 to the outbreak of war.

He made his first appearance in the West End here in his debut performance of *Hamlet*, transferred from the Old Vic in 1930, with Donald Wolfit and Martita Hunt

as Claudius and Gertrude. To see a 25-year-old Prince of Denmark was a novelty for audiences used to seeing middle-aged actors tackling the role. It did well despite the fact that there were two other Hamlets on in London at the same time. (Henry Ainley at the Haymarket, and Alexander Moissi, in German, at the nearby Globe.) Gielgud returned in 1937 in a play especially written for him by Emlyn Williams, titled — curiously to our modern ears – *He Was Born Gay*. It ran for 12 nights. Putting that behind him, he brought in a season of four plays for eight months starting in September of the same year. Gielgud not only played *Richard II* to Michael Redgrave's Bolingbroke, Shylock in *The Merchant Of Venice* to Peggy Ashcroft's Portia, Vershinin in *The Three Sisters* and Joseph Surface in *The School For Scandal*, but also directed the first two.

In addition to the leading actors, Harry Andrews, Dennis Price and Alec Guinness had small parts in all four productions. Redgrave and his wife Rachel Kempson appeared as Charles Surface and Maria in Tyrone Guthrie's *The School For Scandal*, little knowing that their one-year-old daughter Vanessa would one day appear on the same stage with her father in Robert Bolt's *The Tiger And The Horse* (1960), and triumph in Ibsen's *The Lady From The Sea* (1961), and as Nina in *The Seagull* (1964).

Immediately after this exhausting but rewarding season, Gielgud stepped into modern dress to play opposite Marie Tempest in Dodie Smith's family saga *Dear Octopus* (1938). Dame Marie did not get on with the author, and when Dodie took a curtain call on the first night with the company, the actress turned her back on her in full view of the audience. The first night also coincided with Chamberlain's return from Munich. The year's run was broken by the declaration of war, and the Queen's closed down. It reopened in December 1939 with the optimistically titled revue *All Clear* starring Bea Lillie, followed by Daphne du Maurier's *Rebecca* with Owen Nares, Celia Johnson and Margaret Rutherford. It was during the successful run of the latter that the bomb fell.

The devastated theatre stood dark and deserted for almost 20 years, a sad reminder of the blitz, before architects Bryan Westwood and Hugh Casson restored it. It reopened in July 1959, appropriately enough with Sir John Gielgud giving his Shakespeare recital, *The Ages Of Man*. In the same year, the year of his knight-

The young Vanessa Redgrave was Nina in Chekov's
The Seagull in 1964. Peggy Ashcroft (centre)
played Madame Arkadina. (Peter Finch is on the left)
Twenty-one years later, Miss Redgrave graduated
to Arkadina, co-starring with her daughter
Natasha Richardson as Nina

hood, Sir Michael Redgrave returned in *The Aspern Papers*, his own adaptation of the Henry James story. Anthony Newley sang 'What Kind Of Fool Am I?' as Littlechap in the allegorical musical *Stop The World I Want To Get Off* (1961) for over a year before moving with it to Broadway.

The big theatrical event of 1966 was the return of Noël Coward to the West End after a 13-year absence. He starred alongside Irene Worth and Lilli Palmer in a trio of new plays which he gave the omnibus title of *Suite In Three Keys*. Although Coward's health was poor and he often 'dried', he felt 'a warmth and a genuine love emanating from the front of the house at every performance.' It was his final stage appearance. 'The Master' died not long after his friend Marlene Dietrich's successful one-woman show at the Queen's, and Gielgud's starry production of *Private Lives* with the then-married couple, Maggie Smith and Robert Stephens, both in 1972.

The Queen's has housed a small percentage of misses, including Joe Orton's last play, *What The Butler Saw* (1969), in which Sir Ralph Richardson and Coral Browne bravely cavorted, but recent hits such as Alan Bates in *Otherwise Engaged* (1975), Alec Guinness in *The Old Country* (1978), Tom Courtenay in *The Dresser* (1980) and Charlton Heston in *The Caine Mutiny Court Martial* (1985), demonstrate that the Queen's is a theatre of continuing quality.

THE ROYAL COURT

The Establishment-sounding Royal Court Theatre, with its noble brick and stone Italian Renaissance frontage, brazenly stares out on the leafy confines of trendy Sloane Square and the fripperies of the King's Road, Chelsea – a surprising locality in which to find the most radical of all of the great theatres of London, and one that changed the face of British drama in the late 1950s.

Nineteen-fifty-six was the year of the Suez Crisis when Britain was forced to re-examine its role on the world's stage; youth culture such as rock 'n' roll burst onto the scene, and so did the production of *Look Back In Anger* at the Royal Court. 'An angry play by an angry young author . . . neurotic, exaggerated and more than slightly distasteful,' railed *The Daily Mail*, typical of most of the reviews. One critic's voice came through loud and clear – Kenneth Tynan in *The Observer* wrote, 'I doubt if I could love anyone who did not wish to see

Look Back In Anger. It is the best young play of its decade.' Whatever one thought of 27-year-old John Osborne's choleric, wittily rhetorical shout against aspects of British society, it advanced the careers of its author, the director Tony Richardson, and the actors Kenneth Haigh, Alan Bates, and Mary Ure (Osborne's wife-to-be); it gave rise to a movement labelled 'Angry Young Men', and was a landmark in the counterblast against the complacency of the commercial theatre.

The English Stage Company was formed in 1956, with Arts Council subsidy, 'to stage and encourage new writing' under the artistic direction of George Devine

John Osborne's Look Back In Anger *(1956) changed the face of British theatre forever. Here, Jimmy Porter (Kenneth Haigh, right) vents his spleen on his wife Alison (Mary Ure), while friends Cliff and Helena (Alan Bates, Helena Hughes) look on*

'If more plays like tonight's Look Back In Anger are produced, the 'Writer's Theatre' at the Royal Court must surely sink.'

Birmingham Post 1956

(pronounced Deveen). Living up to this pledge, Devine presented a multitude of new works by British writers in the nine years he was at the Court. His achievement was extraordinary. After his death in 1966, the tradition was admirably continued by his successors, William Gaskill, Stuart Burge and Max Stafford-Clark. Among the many notable productions presented over the years have been Osborne's *Luther* (1961), *Inadmissible Evidence* (1964) and *A Patriot For Me* (1965); Arnold Wesker's *Chicken Soup With Barley* (1958), *Roots* (1959), *I'm Talking About Jerusalem* (1960) and *Chips With Everything* (1962); John Arden's *Sergeant Musgrave's Dance* (1959); Ann Jellicoe's *The Knack*

Julie Covington and Tom Wilkinson in Tom And Viv *(1984), Michael Hastings' searing play about T.S. Eliot's first wife, confined to an asylum*

(1962); David Storey's *The Contractor* (1969), *In Celebration* (1969) and *The Changing Room* (1971); Christopher Hampton's *The Philanthropist* (1970) and *Savages* (1973); David Hare's *Teeth 'n' Smiles* (1975); Mary O'Malley's *Once A Catholic* (1977), Nigel Williams' *Class Enemy* (1978), Michael Hastings' *Tom And Viv* (1984); and Caryl Churchill's *Cloud Nine* (1980), *Top Girls* (1982) and *Serious Money* (1987).

Modern foreign greats have not been neglected either, and Brecht, Beckett, Genet, Ionesco and Sartre have been well represented. Even the theatrical knights from the 'other' theatre have not been able to resist the pull of the Royal Court. Sir Alec Guinness played in Ionesco's *Exit The King* (1964) and *Macbeth* (1966); Sir John Gielgud (with Sir Ralph Richardson) in David Storey's *Home* (1970), Charles Wood's *Veterans* (1972) and as Shakespeare in Edward Bond's *Bingo* (1973); and Sir Laurence Olivier in Ionesco's *Rhinoceros* (1960) directed by Orson Welles. After seeing *Look Back In Anger*, Olivier asked Osborne to write a play for him. The result was *The Entertainer* (1957), a triumph in all departments, and a turning point in the great actor's career.

Archie Rice, the fifth-rate comedian Olivier played in *The Entertainer* says, 'Don't clap too hard lady, it's an old building.' In fact, the present building dates from 1888, although there had been a theatre of the same name on the south side of Sloane Square. After that was demolished in 1887, another, designed by Walter Emden and Bertie Crewe, went up on the east side next to the Metropolitan railway station (now Sloane Square tube). Originally a three-tier theatre with a 642-seat capacity, its interior was reconstructed in 1952, closing off the old gallery and reducing the seating to 401. Further redecorations in 1980 enlarged it somewhat. In 1971, a rehearsal room became the 80-seat experimental Theatre Upstairs. Today, the Court's rather unimpressive auditorium, whose sight-lines could be improved, is the strangely antique setting for modern drama that generally preaches change.

Arthur Wing Pinero was the playwright most associated with the Royal Court in its earliest days. His successes here included *The Cabinet Minister* (1890), *The Amazons* (1893), and, particularly, *Trelawny Of The 'Wells'* (1898), which recalled his days as an actor. Also popular was *Under The Clock* (1893), a precursor of intimate revue, in which 22-year-old Seymour Hicks and

The stage – set for Caryl Churchill's Serious Money
(1987), a satire on the Stock exchange

Charles Brookfield impersonated various theatrical luminaries of the day. But the Court's reputation for advanced drama was established when J. E. Vedrenne and Harley Granville-Barker managed the theatre from 1904 to 1907, presenting a remarkable range of plays, 11 of them by George Bernard Shaw, whose wide renown dates from this memorable season. If the spirit of Shaw haunts any theatre, it would surely be the Royal Court. *You Never Can Tell, Man And Superman* and *The Doctor's Dilemma* proved there was a public for intellectual theatre. Not unlike today's Court audience, people came to be stimulated mentally and enjoyed being lectured at. It was Harley Granville-Barker's experience here which led him to espouse the cause of a national theatre.

Shaw returned to the Court, under J. B. Fagan's stewardship, with *Heartbreak House* (1921), his first play since before the war. When Barry Jackson became manager in 1924, he had the courage to present Shaw's mammoth five-part *Back To Methuselah* over four nights. Among Jackson's other achievements were Eden Phillpott's *The Farmer's Wife* (1924), which ran almost three years, and modern dress productions of

Macbeth and *The Taming Of The Shrew* (both 1927). Twenty-one-year-old Laurence Olivier played small roles in the Shakespeare plays. For most of the latter, he had to sit in a stage box in full view of the audience. According to Olivier, he spent much of the time trying to make Ralph Richardson, who played Tranio, laugh. Every night he would pull faces and make gestures to no avail. One night, he did absolutely nothing but stare at Ralph who promptly 'corpsed'. Olivier also appeared in Elmer Rice's expressionist fantasy *The Adding Machine* (1928).

The Royal Court was closed (except for a short period as a cinema) between 1932 and 1952. It then marked time for a few years before the historic arrival of the English Stage Company, which has always invited controversy. There was uproar in some quarters at Edward Bond's *Saved* (1965), which depicted a baby being stoned to death, and the same author's *Early Morning* (1968) presented Queen Victoria as having a lesbian affair with Florence Nightingale. Only on one occasion has the Court been seen to give in to outside pressure. This concerned the last-minute withdrawal of Jim Allen's *Perdition* in 1987, concerning the Holocaust, on the grounds that 'it might offend too many people.' The theatre will no doubt continue to offend and stimulate many people in the future.

THE ROYAL OPERA HOUSE

Opera houses are generally grandiose, luxurious palaces erected to stage the most expensive theatrical art form ever devised – and the Royal Opera House, Covent Garden, can take its place among the world's best. Although less monumental than the Paris Opera or La Scala, its ambience of opulence, enchantment and a sense of occasion is created immediately in the sumptuous lobby. The splendid Grand Staircase on the left rises, between huge allegorical paintings, towards the famous Crush Bar – a great hall with 20-foot high paintings adorning the walls, beneath a sparkling chandelier. All this even before one enters the majestic auditorium, substantially as it was when new in 1858! From the Orchestra Stalls, Stalls Circle and Grand Tier, the horseshoe-shaped levels move up to the Balcony Stalls, and the Valhalla of the Amphitheatre close to the shallow, aquamarine dome. Looking down from this vertiginous height towards the stage, with its famous crimson velvet curtains bearing the Queen's monogram, one notices, above the proscenium, a rustic

scene in which Orpheus plays his lyre. Along the gold tier-fronts stand a bevy of bare-breasted maidens behind rows of claret-shaded candelabra.

The first theatre, on the site of what had been a convent garden (hence the name), was built in 1732 for John Rich, who held the Patent which permitted only the two Theatre Royals, at Drury Lane and Covent Garden, to perform 'legitimate' theatre legitimately. It was originally, therefore, mainly devoted to drama, though three of Handel's operas, *Alcina* (1735), *Atalanta* (1736) and *Berenice* (1737), had their premieres here. Rich, who was constantly in litigation, and who killed a fellow actor in a fight over a wig, managed the theatre until his death in 1761. John Beard, his son-in-law, took over and presented mainly operas until he was succeeded by Thomas Harris in 1774 when plays became the order of the day. Oliver Goldsmith's *She Stoops To Conquer* (1773) and Sheridan's *The Rivals* (1775) had first performances here. In May 1789 Charles Macklin, playing Shylock in *The Merchant Of*

LONDRES
JUIN 1841

*A contemporary engraving of the tragedienne
Rachel at Covent Garden in 1841*

Venice, made his last appearance but, being as old as the century, he failed to complete the performance. In contrast, a tragedian aged only 13 made his London debut in 1804. Master Betty, known as the young Roscius, played the great Shakespearean roles and caused a sensation. Parliament even adjourned in order to see his *Hamlet*. This freakish success ended a year later when his attempt at *Richard III* was hissed off the stage.

In September, 1808, a fire – in which 23 firemen were killed – destroyed the building and Handel's organ and scores with it. A mere 12 months later a new theatre, modelled on the Temple of Minerva at the Acropolis, stood in its place. Owing to the cost of rebuilding, seat prices were raised. This action caused riots and disturbances for 61 nights until, finally, actor-manager John Philip Kemble was forced to lower them again. Kemble's sister, Sarah Siddons, bid farewell to the stage with Lady Macbeth in 1812, and Kemble retired in favour of his younger brother Charles in 1817. Charles Kemble was one of the first actor-managers to bring some historical accuracy to costumes and sets, beginning in 1823 with *King John*, designed by James

Robinson Planché. Planché was also the librettist of Weber's *Oberon* (1826), 'the most important English romantic opera'.

In March 1833, Edmund Kean, playing Othello, was taken ill during a scene with Iago, played by his son, Charles. Falling into Charles' arms, Kean cried, 'Oh God! I am dying . . . speak to them for me.' The greatest actor of the age had made his last exit. One of Kean's rivals was William Charles Macready, who assumed the management of Covent Garden in 1837. He introduced a new calcium light that was to revolutionise stage lighting. 'It was the application of the limelight', wrote Edward Fitzgerald, 'that really threw open the realms of glittering fairyland to the scenic artist.' Macready's reign was marked by internal dissension, and the remarkable Madame Vestris took over in 1839, and the French actress, Rachel, made a memorable appearance in *Horace* in 1841. In 1856, fire once again consumed the Theatre Royal.

On 15 May, 1858, the Royal Italian Opera, the build-

'A very English place for grand occasions! An odd and endearing mixture of red velvet plush and drawing-room intimacy.'

Max Loppert

ing we know today, was opened. Sir Edward M. Barry created an imposing structure in the Roman Renaissance manner with a raised Corinthian portico. The statues by Rossi on either side of the facade, and the Flaxman *bas-reliefs* along the front, survive from the 1809 building. Managed by Frederic Gye, the new premises were given over entirely to operas sung in Italian, regardless of their provenance. Opera at that period was more a social than an artistic event and, as previously, the lights remained on during performances so that the gentry could see and be seen. Berlioz was once refused entry because his evening coat did not match his trousers.

Things improved when Augustus Harris took over in 1888. As operas were now given in their original language and in English, the 'Italian' was dropped from the name of the house. Harris introduced Edouard and Jean de Reszke and Nellie Melba to London, the latter making her debut in *Lucia di Lammermoor* (1888) and continuing to appear in almost every season here until

1914. Adelina Patti sang 25 consecutive seasons in over 30 roles at around £200 a performance.

In the orchestra pit, Gustav Mahler conducted Wagner's *Ring* cycle in 1892 and, in 1908, Hans Richter conducted the first *Ring* in English. Thomas Beecham, backed by his father (Joseph, of pills fame), launched his first season in 1910 with the British premiere of Richard Strauss' *Elektra*. After World War I, during which the opera house was used as a furniture warehouse, Bruno Walter became chief conductor. He concentrated mainly on Wagner, Mozart and Strauss, and his *Der Rosenkavalier* of 1924 (with Lotte Lehmann and Elisabeth Schumann), was a landmark. Beecham returned to take over the baton from 1932 to 1939. Between the wars Italian opera, excepting Puccini's works, was somewhat neglected. For example, not a note of Verdi was heard here for six years.

In 1946 the Covent Garden Opera Company was

David Hockney designed L'Enfant Et Les Sortilége

Mikhail Baryshnikov and Antoinette Sibley in MacMillan's A Month In The Country *in 1985*

formed, subsidised by the Arts Council, and would share the house with the Sadlers Wells Ballet Company run by Ninette de Valois. (Both companies became Royal later). The infant opera company had stormy beginnings, with music director Karl Rankl clashing with the director of productions. The latter was Peter Brook, then only 24 years old, who produced an erotic *Salome*, with sets by Salvador Dali, in 1949. Erich Kleiber contributed greatly to the development of the company between 1950 and 1953. He conducted the first British performance of Alban Berg's *Wozzeck* in 1952. In the same year, Maria Callas made her Covent Garden debut in *Norma*, her grandest tragic role. Highlights of Rafael Kubelik's tenure (1955-1958) were Birgit Nilsson's Brunhilde in the *Ring* (1957), *The Trojans* – given in its entirety for the first time on a single evening, also in 1957 – directed by John Gielgud, and Visconti's production of *Don Carlos* (1958), conducted by Guilini.

English performers, and operas, began to attract attention in the 1950s. There were world premieres of works by native composers such as Benjamin Britten (*Billy Budd*, 1951; *Gloriana*, 1953), William Walton (*Troilus and Cressida*, 1954), and Michael Tippett (*The*

Midsummer Marriage, 1955). The wonderful contralto, Kathleen Ferrier, gave her last ever performance, while in considerable pain, in Gluck's *Orfeo ed Euridice* in 1953. She did not complete the second performance, and was soon dead. In 1959, Australia's Joan Sutherland became a star overnight in *Lucia di Lammermoor*.

When George Solti took over in 1961, he announced his intention of turning Covent Garden into the world's greatest opera house. He almost succeeded, with such triumphs during his regime as *Fidelio* (1961) conducted by Klemperer; *Tosca* (1964) with Callas and Gobbi in a Zeffirelli production, the second act of which is preserved on film for posterity; *Pelléas et Mélisande* (1969); and *Tristan und Isolde* (1971). There were a few failures, too, such as the 1962 *La Forza del Destino*, after which Solti found his car sprayed with the words, 'Solti Go Home'.

It took some time for Colin Davis (1971-1986) to win over the critics and the public. Of the many great

Placido Domingo and Katia Ricciarelli, in the new production of Verdi's Otello (1987)

nights at the opera during his era, mention of two or three must suffice – *The Marriage Of Figaro* in 1971, which brought an unknown young Maori soprano named Kiri Te Kanawa to fame; *La Fanciulla del West* (1980) with sets by James Bond film designer Ken Adam; Berg's *Lulu* in 1981.

Developing parallel to the Royal Opera has been the Royal Ballet, much-travelled and world-renowned. Their reputation took root when the company unveiled the great Margot Fonteyn in *The Sleeping Beauty* to New York audiences in the 1950s. Aside from the traditional classical repertoire – sometimes re-choreographed, as with Rudolph Nureyev's version of *The Nutcracker*, the company's choreographers have enriched the programme with new works too numerous to mention. Examples would include John Cranko's *Pineapple Poll*, Frederick Ashton's *Symphonic Variations*, and Kenneth MacMillan's *Anastasia*, created for the exciting Canadian-born ballerina, Lynne Seymour. Guest choreographers have included the cream of America – Balanchine, Jerome Robbins, Glen Tetley. All have been served by superlative dancers, among them Fonteyn, Michael Somes, Nadia Nerina, David Blair, Merle Park, Donald Macleary, Antoinette Sibley, Anthony Dowell, Lesley Collier, Wayne Eagling and Stephen Jefferies. Svetlana Beriosova, Nureyev himself, and his natural successor Mikhail Baryshnikov, have also enhanced this great company.

'Working conditions here are worse than any other great opera house in the world', writes Clive Boursnell in his book on the Royal Opera House. For years it suffered from poor ventilation backstage, and lack of dressing room and rehearsal space. Despite the extension built in 1982, it faces horrendous problems of space and finance, but a major reconstruction and renovation programme – for the theatre itself and its precincts – is already under way. This will be of great benefit to the building, but its immediate neighbours stand to suffer. General Administrator Jeremy Isaacs and musical director Bernard Haitink will have to wrestle with these problems over the next few years to make sure of a rosy future for this national – and international – treasure.

SADLER'S WELLS

The world of tutus and tights, pirouettes and *pas-de-deux* is conjured up for most people when Sadler's Wells is mentioned, mainly because of the years between 1931 and 1940 that the Vic-Wells (later the Sadler's Wells) Ballet Company spent at the building where the hitherto undreamed-of English Ballet was born. Until then, dancers had to change their names to foreign ones to gain acceptance. It was here, in the north London suburb of Islington, far from the madding West End crowds, that a permanent ballet company was formed. It was created by the formidable Lilian Baylis of the Old Vic, who spent five years raising the money to build the theatre after demolishing the old one, and rapidly went from strength to strength, so that the 'Wells' became known throughout the land. Installed since 1946 at the Royal Opera House, Covent Garden, the company has perpetuated the name in its official title – the Sadler's Wells Royal Ballet.

Ironically, this temple to Terpsichore – the theatre that housed (and still houses) an art of grace, beauty and physical dexterity – is itself much lacking in these qualities. Yet this large, shapeless brick building with its cinema-type canopy and arched window above it to relieve the monotony of the exterior, is held in great affection by the multitudes of balletomanes and opera lovers who so often took the underground to Angel in order to enter an artistic heaven. Memories of glorious nights still hang over the genial foyer and circle bar, and even in the functional 1499-seat auditorium designed by F.G.M. Chancellor. But, as John Earl points out, it is a listed building mainly 'for its archaeology rather than its architecture.'

The name derives from the medicinal spring that was discovered in the grounds of a Mr Thomas Sadler in the year 1683. (The original well can be found under a trap door at the back of the stalls.) The land, then in the open country, became a popular pleasure garden where people could watch various entertainments and

One of the attractive, recently refurbished bars

take the waters. A wooden 'Musick House' was erected where concerts and masques could be given. It stood for nearly a century, until a stone theatre was built in its place in 1765 by Thomas Rosoman, who became manager. Tom King, the well-known Drury Lane actor and creator of the role of Sir Peter Teazle, succeeded him in 1772, remaining for 10 years until Henry Siddons (the actress Sarah Siddons' husband), in association with dramatist-actor-composer Charles Dibdin and his two sons, took over over. In 1801, a small boy called Master Carey performed here, before becoming Edmund Kean in adulthood.

'Nautical Drama' drew the crowds to Islington from 1814, when a tank of water, 90-foot long and 3-foot deep, was placed on the stage in order to simulate naval battles. Swimmers manipulated scale-model ships while cannons fired in plays called *The Siege of Gibraltar* and *Naval Triumph; Or, The Tars Of Old England*. However, with the breaking of the monopoly of the Patent Theatres in 1843, which prevented legitimate drama being given other than at the Theatres Royal, a new era dawned at Sadler's Wells. The superb actor-manager Samuel Phelps took a lease on the near-derelict building in 1844 where, in the following 18 years, he produced almost all of Shakespeare's plays, thus making it 'a place for justly representing the works of our great dramatic poet,' as Phelps rightly claimed. For the first time, the location which started as a spa became an oasis of culture.

But 'Oh! What a fall was there!' when Phelps retired in 1862. The theatre was used as a skating rink and a prize-fighting venue before it was closed for repairs in 1878. A year later it was bought by Mrs Bateman, the widow of the owner of the Lyceum. On her death in 1881, it passed into her daughter Isabel's hands. Unfortunately, the theatre developed into the home of crude melodrama where the 'gallery contained the most villainous, desperate, hatchet-faced assembly of ruffians to be found in all London.' No wonder Miss Bateman left the stage to take Holy Orders. The 'Wells' later became a music hall, then an early cinema before closing down in 1906 where it lay, like Aurora in the ballet *The Sleeping Beauty*, until Lilian Baylis hacked her way through the tangled financial undergrowth to kiss it into life again.

At first, drama, ballet and opera alternated between the Old Vic and Sadler's Wells. The opening Shakespeare season of 1931-1932, in which John Gielgud played Malvolio, Benedick and King Lear, and Ralph Richardson was Sir Toby Belch, Petruchio, Bottom and Henry V, ran two weeks at the 'Vic' and one at the 'Wells'. But this proved too expensive and in 1935 only

'To return to Sadlers Wells for any performance holds all the excitement of the old days.'

Ninette de Valois, 1978

opera and ballet were given, while drama remained at the Vic. With the help of Nicolas Sergueyev from the Russian Maryinsky, the ballet company, under Ninette de Valois (born Edris Stannus in 1898), was able to build up a classical repertoire that included *Giselle, Swan Lake, Coppelia* and *The Nutcracker*, and there were new ballets commissioned from British choreographers. Frederick Ashton delivered *Facade* (1931), *Apparitions* (1936), *Les Patineurs* (1937) and *Horoscope* (1938), while de Valois choreographed *Job* (1931), *The Rake's Progress* and *Checkmate* (both 1935), most of them still performed. When the leading dancers Alicia Markova (Alice Marks) and Anton Dolin (Patrick Healey-Kay) left to form their own company, Margot Fonteyn (Peggy Hookham) and Robert Helpmann (Robert Helpmann) stepped into their ballet shoes. The opera company took a little longer to gain wide recognition, but under the baton of Laurence Collingwood, and with singers such as Joan Cross, Edith Coates, Tudor Davies and Henry Wendon, and a growing reper-

toire strong on Wagner and Verdi sung in English, it soon blossomed.

In 1938, the year after the parsimonious Baylis died, improvements were carried out by enlarging the stage, and building new dressing rooms and a rehearsal room. However, in 1940, the theatre was damaged by an enemy bomb and performances were held at the New Theatre (now the Albery) during the war. Only the opera company returned to its home at Sadler's Wells in 1945 with an historic reopening, the world premiere of Benjamin Britten's *Peter Grimes* with Peter Pears in the title role and Reginald Goodall in the pit. It heralded a new dawn of English opera. Over the years, especially under Norman Tucker from 1948 to 1966, the Sadler's Wells opera grew into a real ensemble, members of which were conductors Alexander Gibson and Colin Davis, producers Denis Arundell, Wendy Toye,

A venue for international art, The Wells presented the Japanese Noh Theatre in 1983

Famous mime Lindsay Kemp in Flowers *(1985)*

Basil Coleman and Glen Byam Shaw, and singers who became internationally famous such as Amy Shuard, David Ward, Peter Glossop, Donald McIntyre, Norman Bailey and Rita Hunter. In 1959, the doubtful acoustics were improved by means of a canopy suspended over the proscenium.

After the company moved to the Coliseum in 1974 to become the English National Opera, the theatre fell on less exciting times. But opera and ballet still live on here, the renowned building providing a showcase for visiting companies such as the Handel Operatic Society, the New Opera Company, the London Contemporary Dance Company and many prestigious and exciting foreign troupes. Despite a continual struggle with finance, Islington's Angel continues to watch over the 'Wells'.

David Gordon's Pick-Up Company in 1985

THE ST. MARTIN'S

They make an odd couple, the sober St Martin's and the more frivolous Ambassadors, a few yards from each other, separated in space by Tower Court and in time by the First World War. The pre-war Ambassadors has a richly adorned interior while the post-war St Martin's avoided fancy plasterwork, opting for the polished wood of the balustraded balcony fronts and Doric columns on pedestals at balcony level, making it seem less intimate than the 550-seat capacity would suggest. Classicism is maintained by the six giant attached Ionic columns, framing three storeys of large windows, on the stone facade. Links between the two theatres are the same architect, W. G. R. Sprague, the fact that C. B. Cochran was a lessee of both at their beginnings, and *The Mousetrap*, which ran for 22 years at the Ambassadors then moved next door to the St Martin's in 1974 for a further interminable run.

The theatre that started off on a light note in August 1916 with Gaiety Girl Gertie Millar in Cochran's *Houp La!*, soon plunged into the gloom of Eugene Brieux's *Damaged Goods* in the same year. The play, a study of VD, caused a sensation. After a couple of musical comedies, the theatre returned to 'serious' business with 62-year-old Sir Frank Benson as *Hamlet* (1920). The director Tyrone Guthrie noted that 'He'd been a very handsome man and proud of his fine physique. It was sad to see this rouged, gaunt ruin of masculine beauty pretending to be Hamlet.'

When the St Martin's was brought under the management of Alec Rea and Basil Dean in 1920, an enterprising series of modern plays was produced. Among the more established writers, John Galsworthy was represented by *The Skin Game* (1920), *Loyalties* (1922) and *The Forest* (1924); Karel Capek's satire on modern regimentation, *R. U. R.* (1923) made an impact, as did Frederick Lonsdale's *Spring Cleaning* (1925), which had people raising their hands in horror at a 'street walker' being among the *dramatis personae*. Less con-

> *'Alfred Butt instructed his lieutenants to get the pick of my girls from the St Martin's, even if they cost double the salary of the ordinary chorus girl.'*
>
> Charles B. Cochran, 1925

troversial was Noel Coward's cardboard Ruritanian drama, *The Queen Was In The Parlour* (1926) with Madge Titheradge, Herbert Marshall and Lady Tree.

Clemence Dane's first play, *A Bill Of Divorcement*, which dealt with the problem of divorce on grounds of insanity, featured a promising young actress called Meggie Albanesi in the role that first brought Katharine Hepburn film fame. Sadly, Miss Albanesi died two years later aged 24, her death being commemorated by a plaque in the foyer of the theatre. Another young actress, 17-year-old Hermione Baddeley, scored a triumph as Florrie Small in Charles McEvoy's study of East End slum life, *The Likes Of Her* (1923). The Great War was the subject of *The White Chateau* (1927) written by Reginald Berkeley while recovering from wounds he received at the front.

The St Martin's continued its policy of dramas on

contemporary issues into the 1930s with John Gielgud directing his first modern play, Rodney Ackland's *Strange Orchestra*. Unfortunately, Mrs Patrick Campbell left, after rehearsing for some weeks, because her dog was in quarantine. Of *The Green Bay Tree* (1933) by Mordaunt Shairp, featuring Hugh Williams and Frank Vosper, the critic of *The Star* wrote, 'If the object was to arouse powerful detestation of two abominable people a kind of success may be concluded, but that is all.' The play is possibly the first contemporary drama on the subject of homosexuality, although the word itself is never used.

The first production of J. B. Priestley's oft-revived Yorkshire comedy, *When We Are Married* (1938) was given here, directed by Basil Dean. The author himself took over the role of Henry Ormonroyd, the pickled photographer, when Frank Pettingell was injured in a road accident. He played it for several nights to great applause. Its run was terminated by the outbreak of

The Mousetrap lives on. Here is the 1986/87 cast

The intimate yet imposing wood-panelled interior

war. Productions came and went like buses for some years until Edward Percy's murder tale, *The Shop At Sly Corner* (1945), ran 863 performances.

Successes in the 50s and 60s were Joyce Grenfell in the revue *Penny Plain* (1951), American actress Geraldine Page in *The Rainmaker* (1956), two plays by Hugh and Margaret Williams, *Plaintiff In A Pretty Hat* (1957) and *The Grass Is Greener* (1958), *Guilty Party* (1961), *Where Angels Fear To Tread* (1963) from the E. M. Forster novel, and Eric Portman in *The Creeper* (1965). In preparation for the long years of *The Mousetrap*, Keith Baxter, Anthony Quayle and 'many others' starred in Anthony Shaffer's clever thriller *Sleuth* (1970) for three years. Presumably, the news of 'whodunnit' in Agatha Christie's *The Mousetrap*, in its 35th year, has not reached the eager people buying their tickets at the St Martin's.

Keith Baxter (left) and Anthony Quayle in Anthony Shaffer's ingenious Sleuth *(1970)*

THE SAVOY

The Savoy Theatre, built for impresario Richard D'Oyly Carte from the profits he accrued from Gilbert and Sullivan's light operas, was the very model of a modern major theatre when it opened in October 1881. As *The Times* stated, 'This is the first time that it has been attempted to light any public building entirely by electricity. What is being done is an experiment, and may succeed or fail.' At the opening production, the 170th performance of *Patience*, the electric lights were 'cheered to the very echo.' People have been cheering at the Savoy ever since.

D'Oyly Carte, who had instigated the partnership of W. S. Gilbert and Arthur Sullivan, dreamed of building his own theatre in which to stage their works. A suitable site was found close to the Thames Embankment within the grounds of the old Savoy Palace Hotel, and a theatre, designed by C. J. Phipps, was constructed within a few months. Not only by the 'application of electric light for theatrical purposes', was the Savoy in advance of other theatres of the day. Not for D'Oyly Carte the 'Gingerbread School of Decorative Art' with its elaborate ornamentation and paintings of cherubs and the like. The decoration was of cleaner lines, and delicate colouring.

The first years were given over almost exclusively to Gilbert and Sullivan's works, which became known as the Savoy operas: *Iolanthe* (1882), *Princess Ida* (1884), *The Mikado* (1885), *Ruddigore* (1887), *The Yeoman Of The Guard* (1888) and *The Gondoliers* (1889) all had first performances here. During the run of the latter, the irascible Gilbert (lyrics) quarrelled with Sullivan (music) and they refused to work with each other again. Sir Arthur, therefore, collaborated with Sydney Grundy on *Haddon Hall* (1892) before the celebrated duo were reconciled. Their thirteenth operetta together, *Utopia Limited* (1893), failed by trying to hit too many targets in Victorian England at once. Their last work as a team was *The Grand Duke* (1896), also a

> *'The new Savoy Theatre is the first really outstanding example of modern decoration applied to a public place on a commercial basis.'*

Country Life 1929

A poster of the period advertises Gilbert and Sullivan's Princess Ida

failure. It marked the end of an era, but not the end of Gilbert and Sullivan at the Savoy. There were seasons of revivals in 1929-1930, 1932-1933, 1961-1962, and two weeks in 1975 celebrating the centenary of their first success, *Trial By Jury*. Full-length portraits of Gilbert and Sullivan stand in the theatre today as a memento of their splendid reign.

In contrast to the melodious music of Sullivan and the witty libretti of Gilbert were Harley Granville-Barker's epoch-making Shakespeare productions between 1912 and 1914. John Gielgud recollected in *A Midsummer Night's Dream*, 'the gold-painted fairies, the swaying green curtains to suggest the wood, the hanging canopy overhead – a kind of chandelier of white and green – and the slim tall figure of Oberon, my cousin Dennis Neilson-Terry. I recall also the slightly bewildered reactions of the audience.' The simple and abstract staging, in contrast to Tree's lavish productions at His Majesty's, received much abuse. Barker's wife, Lillah McCarthy, played Helena, Viola in *Twelfth Night*, and Hermione to Henry Ainley's Leontes in *The Winter's Tale* of whom critic W. A. Darlington commented, 'my first experience of really passionate acting, and it convinced me once and for all that the theatre's first concern was with emotion.'

Between the wars, Gertrude Page's *Paddy The Next Best Thing* (1920) ran for over two years, while Noel

Coward's second play, *The Young Idea*, (1923) featuring himself, ran only eight weeks causing Noel to remark, 'London is outraged at the play coming off, everyone is talking about it and it's doing me a lot of good.' Playwright John Van Druten first came to prominence with *Young Woodley* (1928), a study of a schoolboy's infatuation with his teacher's wife, which had unaccountably been banned previously. In 1929 a first play by a then unknown playwright, R. C. Sherriff, a moving and realistic portrayal of men in the trenches called *Journey's End*, was an immediate success. It led to the Hollywood careers of both the director James Whale and the actor Colin Clive. Laurence Olivier, who had created the role of Captain Stanhope in Sunday performances, opted to play in *Beau Geste*, which flopped. After *Journey's End* transferred, the whole of the interior and part of the exterior of the theatre was rebuilt.

The main entrance was shifted from the Embankment side (where the old Phipps facade is still visible) to the courtyard of the new Savoy Hotel. In keeping with the hotel's frontage of stainless steel with its knight in shining armour above the entrance, the theatre decked itself in silver splendour. The interior, designed by Frank A. Tugwell and Basil Ionides, is an Art Deco delight. Many exquisite details on doors, seats and walls, a glass screen in the Circle Bar, a group of Egyptian maidens round a large vase, and golden Japanese scenes on either side of the stage, give it all an air of chic. Winston Churchill, a constant visitor, would always have a seat in the Royal Box. This was built out for him slightly, thus obscuring a few seats on the side of the circle. When his hearing deteriorated, he would sit in the front row. The Savoy remains one of the few London theatres to still have a box at the back of the circle.

The hits of the World War II years were Kaufman and Hart's wicked comedy, *The Man Who Came To Dinner* (1941), in which Robert Morley played Sheridan Whiteside. (The actor's son, critic Sheridan Morley, was named after the character.) Coral Browne was also in it, as well as starring in *My Sister Eileen* (1943), *The Last of Mrs Cheyney* (1944) and *Lady Frederick* (1946). Post-war, Margaret Lockwood appeared in Agatha Christie's *The Spider's Web* (1954) for over two years,

The art deco foyer and stairs to the stalls; Egyptian maidens inhabit the onyx urns

STALLS

DRESS
CIRCLE

STALLS   DRESS
                CIRCLE

FOR SECURITY
REASONS PLEASE
LEAVE ALL PACKAGES
AND BAGS IN
THE CLOAKROOM

Paul Eddington, Jan Waters and Patricia Routledge in Michael Frayn's hilarious look at theatre folk, Noises Off

and in *Subway In The Sky* (1957). Noel Coward renewed his acquaintance with the Savoy with his musical *Sail Away* (1962) in which Elaine Stritch as Mimi Paragon first made herself known to British audiences. *High Spirits* (1964), a musical adaptation of Coward's play *Blithe Spirit* by Hugh Martin and Timothy Gray, limped along for three months, but the Savoy would soon have a string of long runs: with plays like *Alibi For A Judge* (1965), two William Douglas Home comedies, *The Secretary Bird* (1968), and *Lloyd George Knew My Father* (1972) with Ralph Richardson and Peggy Ashcroft (replaced by Celia Johnson), and the controversial *Whose Life Is It Anyway?* with Tom Conti in 1978. Michael Frayn's farce of the theatre, *Noises Off* (1982), ran for over four years – a far cry from Gilbert and Sullivan, but just as entertaining, in a theatre renowned for sheer entertainment.

THE SHAFTESBURY

On 19 July 1973, just as the Shaftesbury Theatre was about to celebrate the 2000th performance of the 'flower children' musical *Hair*, part of the ceiling of the auditorium fell in. It seemed as though the theatre's days were numbered as the threat of turning it into an office block loomed over its little roof tower. Would demolition workers really knock down Bertie Crewe's stone frontage that had dominated the corner at the junction of Shaftesbury Avenue and High Holborn since 1911? Would anyone have the heart to wreck the florid interior, with its eight bow-fronted boxes framed by giant Ionic columns? Would a hammer be taken to the life-size statues representing Comedy, Tragedy, Poetry and Music that sit over each upper box? How could the *bas-relief* of reclining women and Roman soldiers over the proscenium be shattered without compunction? Members of the entertainment industry and Equity, the actors' union, fought a vigorous compaign to keep the theatre open by organizing protest marches and getting petitions signed. Happily, in March 1974, the Department of the Environment gave in to the

pressure and placed the Shaftesbury on the Statutory List of Buildings of Special Architectural or Historic Interest. Like one of the heroines in the melodramas for which it was built, this pretty Edwardian theatre was saved from a terrible fate in the nick of time.

Under the management of the brothers Walter and Frederick Melville, the New Princes Theatre (as it was originally called until it became the Princes in 1914) housed a series of popular melodramas that have since come to dust. Seymour Hicks' three-year reign began in 1916 with a revival of *Bluebell In Fairyland*. In 1919, C. B. Cochran took over for a while, the year the great soprano Maggie Teyte appeared in André Messager's light opera *Monsieur Beaucaire*. The Princes also played host to the D'Oyly Carte Opera Company when the Savoy was unavailable. Seasons of the works of Gilbert and Sullivan were presented here in the 20s, 40s and 50s. In fact, the large auditorium of 1250 (now 1305) seats has always been suitable for operettas, musicals and ballets. Diaghilev's Russian ballet performed here in 1921 and 1927, and Sadler's Wells Op-

> *'This particular theatre, because of the ambience of the auditorium . . . provides an intimate relationship between performer and audience, so necessary for comedy.'*
>
> Ray Cooney

era and Ballet Company in 1944.

Among the straight plays were *Daniel* (1921), in which Sarah Bernhardt made her final London appearance; *Alf's Button* (1924), a fantasy written by the theatre critic W. A. Darlington; and *Macbeth* (1926), starring Sybil Thorndike and Henry Ainley as the murderous Scottish couple. A gas-pipe explosion in a nearby street interrupted the run of George Gershwin's *Funny Face* (1928), featuring Fred and Adele Astaire and Leslie Henson. Due to 'the impassability of the roadway to vehicular traffic', the theatre was closed for some weeks. In 1929, Firth Shephard blew in as manager, remaining until 1946. The shows under his aegis included Sardou's *Diplomacy* (1933), two adaptations from stories by Edgar Wallace, *The Frog* (1936) and *The Gusher* (1937), and John O'Keeffe's 1791 comedy *Wild Oats* (1938). Although the theatre suffered some bomb blasts in 1940 and 1941, it managed to remain open during the war years.

Ironically, it was in the post-war days that the Princes was dark more often than not. Bright spots were *His Excellency* (1950) with Eric Portman; Michael Redgrave and Peggy Ashcroft as *Antony And Cleopatra* (1953) from Stratford-On-Avon; the American musicals *Pal Joey* (1954) and *Wonderful Town* (1955), and a British one *Summer Song* (1956), based on the music and life of Dvorak. When the partnership of Charles Clore and EMI bought the theatre in 1962, it was redecorated and renamed the Shaftesbury. Frank Loesser's Broadway hit musical *How To Succeed In Business Without Really Trying* (1963), did for the box office what the title suggests. In contrast Lionel Bart's Robin Hood musical *Twang!* (1965) ran for a mere 43 performances. After that, Eric Sykes and Jimmy Edwards in *Big Bad Mouse* (1966) kept the coach parties happy for over a year before the advent of *Hair* in 1968.

Hair was the musical that gave voice to hippiedom, to the anti-Vietnam war and Civil Rights movements, and that opened the day after theatre censorship of-

Run For Your Wife *was one of the Theatre of Comedy's biggest hits, here and at the Criterion. L to R: Eric Sykes, Ian Ogilvie, Stratford Johns, Carole Hawkins and James Bolam*

The seminal American 'hippy' musical Hair *made its English home at the Shaftesbury*

ficially ended, thus allowing audiences the sight of full frontal nudity, both male and female.

After its escape from the bulldozers, the Shaftesbury continued to present musicals, notably Neil Simon and Marvin Hamlisch's *They're Playing Our Song* (1980). In 1986 the theatre had another facelift. It now has a bright and attractive lobby with an array of flowers placed in small alcoves, and the auditorium is a delightful wedding cake of pink and white. It was two years earlier that the Theatre of Comedy company, founded by writer-director Ray Cooney and supported by 30 leading actors, writers and directors, bought the theatre and renamed it, officially, the Shaftesbury Theatre of Comedy.

The company, unique in being a co-operative commercial venture run only by members of the theatrical profession, includes among its founder members John Alderton and his wife Pauline Collins, Richard Briers, Tom Conti, Tom Courtenay, Jim Dale, Judi Dench, Nigel Hawthorne, Maureen Lipman, Geraldine McEwan, Julia McKenzie, John Mortimer and Donald Sinden. One of its chief aims, besides presenting comedies both old and new, is 'to consider as paramount the service and comfort of the audience'. Among the company's successes at the Shaftesbury have been Peter O'Toole in *Pygmalion* and Donald Sinden in Ray Cooney's farce, *Two Into One* (both 1984). A gutsy character in Stephen Sondheim's *Follies* (1987) sings, 'I'm Still here'. The same claim can be made by this lovely theatre.

THE STRAND

Looking at this solid, classical, corner building with its giant columns and pediments, it is difficult to imagine that the Strand was actually bombed in both World Wars. In each case it continued to function as if nothing had happened. In 1915, during a performance of *The Scarlet Pimpernel*, it suffered a Zeppelin raid. Fred Terry, John Gielgud's great-uncle and an actor-manager in the grand manner, went down among the audience in his Sir Percy Blakeney costume, urging them not to be afraid, before stepping back onto the stage and continuing with the play. During Donald Wolfit's Shakespeare season in October 1940, a German bomb fell on the theatre damaging the dressing rooms. After having dug out the costumes from the debris, the actors clambered over the ruins to get to the stage. These are two of the most extraordinary examples of the dictum, 'The show must go on.'

Shows have been going on at the Strand non-stop since it opened, in May 1905, with a season of operas alternating with plays given in Italian by the remarkable tragedienne Eleonora Duse and her company. In the same year, a crack in the proscenium arch of his own theatre drove Herbert Beerbohm Tree to bring in *Oliver Twist*, starring himself as Fagin, while it was being repaired. Tree would have found the Waldorf (as the Strand was first called) no less luxurious than His Majesty's. It was built at the same time and with an almost identical facade to the Aldwych Theatre on the opposite corner, separated by the Waldorf Hotel, the architect of both theatres being the renowned W. G. R. Sprague. Although lacking the delightful oval gallery of its near neighbour, the interior decorations of the Strand are far more impressive.

At the foot of the elegant stairway are twin female

Detail of sculptural ornamentation in auditorium

165

The renowned Italian tragedienne Eleanora Duse graced the Strand with her acclaimed presence

figurines holding lamps which throw light upon the highly polished brass railings and marble walls. In the green and gold 927-seat auditorium are two tiers of boxes, framed in Ionic pilasters and crowned with an ornate sculptural group of cupids. More cupids attend the Sun God in a chariot pulled by four horses, in a vigorous and colourful design above the stage. On the circular ceiling are painted allegorical figures after Le Brun. The Royal Box, used mainly by businessmen wishing to impress their clients or girlfriends, has a large retiring room.

In the years before World War I, apart from Tree and La Duse, many of the great names of the Edwardian theatre appeared at the Strand. H. B. Irving in *Lights Out* (1905), Cyril Maude in *She Stoops to Conquer* (1906), and E. H. Sothern and his wife Julia Marlowe in four Shakespeare plays. Matheson Lang gave the theatre its first long run (403 performances) with *Mr Wu*'(1913). So identified did Lang become with the title role that he called his autobiography of 1940 'Mr Wu Looks Back'. During the war, it was the visit of Fred

Terry and Julia Neilson in *Henry Of Navarre, Sweet Nell Of Old Drury* and *The Scarlet Pimpernel* that held audiences in rapture.

Arthur Bourchier, whose portrait hangs in the foyer, ran the theatre for eight years from 1919. Among his successes were a dramatization of *Treasure Island*, presented every Christmas from 1922 to 1926; the first British production of Eugene O'Neill's 1903 play *Anna Christie* (1923) with Pauline Lord in the title role; and another American import, *Broadway* (1926) by Philip Dunning and George Abbott. When Bourchier died while touring South Africa in 1927, George Grossmith took over for a couple of years during which he produced Charles Laughton (a year before his film debut) in *Beauty*, and Miriam Hopkins (three years prior to her Hollywood career) in *Bachelor Father* (both 1927).

While farces were still packing them in a few yards away at the Aldwych, comedian Leslie Henson and Firth Shephard produced a rival series of similar entertainments with titles such as *It's A Boy!* (1930), *It's A Girl!* and *Night Of The Garter* (both 1932). After a year's run of *1066 And All That* (1935), 'a comic history with music', farce returned with Aldwych favourites Robertson 'Oh Calamity' Hare and Alfred Drayton in Vernon Sylvaine's *Aren't Men Beasts* (1936) and *A Spot Of Bother* (1937); and Ben Travers' *Banana Ridge* (1938) and *Spotted Dick* (1939).

For most of the war years from 1942, Joseph Kesselring's black comedy *Arsenic And Old Lace*, with Lilian Braithwaite (created a Dame in 1943 during the run), Mary Jerrold, Frank Pettingell and Naunton Wayne, occupied the large Strand. One night, after the performance, Dame Lilian had to take refuge in the ground floor cloakroom during an air-raid that lasted many hours. Asked if she was exhausted by the episode, she replied, 'Certainly not! We were fifty pounds up last night.' Braithwaite, the mother of actress Joyce Carey, had been at the Strand 29 years previously in *Mr Wu*.

If the Strand managed to withstand the bombs of two world wars, then the booming tones of Peggy Mount as Emma Hornett, the battle-axe mother-in-law-to-be in *Sailor Beware* (1955), shook its very foundations for over three years. The 40-year-old actress, who had spent years in provincial rep, suddenly found herself a West End star. Aside from a satirical revue, *For Adults Only* (1958), and *The Affair* (1961), an adaptation of C. P. Snow's novel, shows came and went with rapidity for

*'This mass exhumation of former film stars –
British at that – was regarded by the critics as
turning the Strand into a disaster area.'*

Michael Denison 1965

a few years. One such was *The Princess* (1960) which
got such bad notices that the management offered free
seats for a week. The experiment failed.

The opening night of *A Funny Thing Happened On
The Way To The Forum* in November 1963 co-incided
with the news of the assassination of John F. Kennedy.
The audience was not much in the mood for laughter,
but the musical Roman romp, starring Frankie
Howerd, and Robertson Hare as a slave called Erronius,
overcame the initial resistance, and the show ran
nearly two years.

Alastair Sim and Dora Bryan in Shaw's *Too True To
Be Good* and Margaret Lockwood and Richard Todd in
Wilde's *An Ideal Husband* (both 1965) breezed through

Stairs from foyer to dress circle

Felicity Kendal and Roger Rees starred in The Real
Thing *(1982), Tom Stoppard's highly successful
play about contemporary marriage*

on their way to other theatres. Peggy Mount returned
to the scene of her first triumph in J. B. Priestley's
When We Are Married (1970), before the incredible run
– 11 years – of the farce, *No Sex Please We're British*
(1971), by Anthony Marriott and Alistair Foot. The play
received a rave from 'serious' *Sunday Times* critic
Harold Hobson, who singled out young Michael Crawford for special mention. Like *The Mousetrap*, it virtually became a national institution and continued to run
and run. When it left for the Garrick and then the
Duchess, Tom Stoppard's *The Real Thing* (1984) was
able to attract the crowds. *Cabaret* (1986) which followed, with dancer Wayne Sleep as the M. C., was ended
a year later by a musicians' strike – another bombshell
delivered to this survivor of a theatre.

THE VAUDEVILLE

This refined, discreet, small theatre in the Strand can lay claim to having launched Henry Irving on his way to becoming the dominant actor-manager during the last 30 years of Queen Victoria's reign. The first theatre on the site was built in 1870 by C. J. Phipps for three of the most popular actors of the day: David James, H. J. Montague and Thomas Thorne, known as the Jew, the Gent and the Gentile. They offered the 32-year-old Irving ten pounds a week to join the company and appear in the opening production, *For Love Or Money*. During the run, he was asked by budding playwright James Albery (the same age as Irving) to read the manuscript of his play *Two Roses*, 'a dainty domestic comedy'. Irving, who had been typecast for years as a villain in trashy plays, was worried that David James (the uncle of David Belasco) might claim the comic role for himself. In the event, Irving played the part of Digby Grant for 15 months before the American impresario, the self-styled Colonel Bateman, installed him at his newly-bought Lyceum Theatre (now a dance hall) round the corner. It was there that Irving made theatrical history.

In 1871, Montague (who was to die two years later aged 34) left the Vaudeville in the hands of his partners. They broke all previous records with H. J. Byron's comedy *Our Boys* (1875), which ran four years. Its popularity was so phenomenal that Strand omnibuses would pull up outside the Vaudeville and the conductors would shout, 'Our Boys!' It was immediately followed by the distaff version called *Our Girls* (1879), which failed. Lightweight entertainments were the main fare, indeed have been throughout most of the theatre's existence, interrupted by Henry Arthur Jones' 'problem play' *Saints And Sinners* (1884), which shocked some people with its 'religious blasphemies'. The charming Cyril Maude, then in his 20s, redressed the balance by appearing in a series of comedies from 1888 until the theatre was reconstructed in 1891.

Foyer detail. The bust is that of Shakespeare

'This little jewel-box of a theatre has, unfortunately, over recent years contained more paste than gems.'

Clive Hirschhorn, 1986

Sir Seymour Hicks in Quality Street

The compact four-storey Portland stone exterior, with its first-level loggia and French casement windows, could well have passed for the private house of a wealthy Victorian merchant. Today, the facade can be appreciated in its entirety because it only has a small sign over the canopy. Thomas Thorne, the remaining member of the original trio, sold the Vaudeville to the brothers Gatti, whose family continued to own it until 1969. From 1900 to 1906, Agostino and Stephano Gatti shared the management with Charles Frohman, who presented a string of successes starring Seymour Hicks and his wife Ellaline Terriss including *Bluebell In Fairyland* (1901) and J. M. Barrie's *Quality Street* (1902). The couple's last appearance at the Vaudeville was in *The Belle Of Mayfair* (1906) before they moved on to the Aldwych built for them and Frohman. Charles Hawtrey (father of the comedian in the 'Carry On' films) carried on the tradition in several comedies.

For ten years from 1915, the Vaudeville was the home of the Charlot revues. André Charlot had made a name for himself previously as a specialist of the genre at the Alhambra, a famous music hall demolished in 1936. (The Odeon Cinema, Leicester Square, now stands on the site.) Most of the Vaudeville revues had one word titles like *Samples* (1915), *Some* (1916), *Cheep* (1917), *Tabs* (1918), *Snap* (1922), and *Yes* (1923), and were instrumental in helping the careers of Bea Lillie, Gertrude Lawrence, Binnie Hale and Stanley Lupino (father of film actress-director Ida Lupino).

In 1926, the theatre was given a completely new interior, keeping the 1892 Phipps frontage intact. The proscenium was enlarged, new stairways built and the auditorium changed from its horseshoe shape to that of a rectangle with classical ornamentation. It then resumed where it left off – with revues from *Vaudeville Vanities* (1926) to *Charlot's Non-Stop Revue* (1937).

A 1920s poster for a Charlot revue

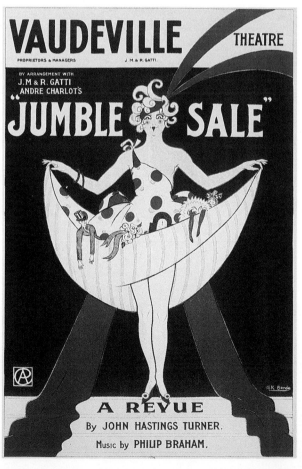

Revue departed, another redecoration ensued, and in came Robert Morley's second play *Goodness, How Sad!* (1938). The wartime successes were three plays by women – *Men In Shadow* (1942) by Mary Hayley Bell, starring her husband John Mills; Enid Bagnold's first play *Lottie Dundass* (1943); and Esther McCracken's *No Medals* (1944), which ran 742 performances.

In 1947, William Douglas Home (brother of future Prime Minister Alec Douglas Home) made a name for himself with the high-life comedy *The Chiltern Hundreds*, which ran for over two years with 78-year-old A. E. Matthews playing a dotty earl. The next long run, in fact the longest in Britain since *Chu Chin Chow*, was a whimsical little English musical by Julian Slade and Dorothy Reynolds called *Salad Days* (1954). Its tinkly

Left to right: Patricia Hodge, Tim Pigott-Smith, Oliver Cotton and Brenda Blethyn in Michael Frayn's Benefactors *(1984)*

but pleasant tunes kept audiences happy for six years. The same authors tried to repeat their success with *Follow That Girl* (1960) and *Wildest Dreams* (1961), but public taste had changed. In 1962, the Vaudeville, known mostly for traditional entertainment, had its first whiff of the 'Angry Young Man' school of drama when Arnold Wesker's class-battle air-force play *Chips With Everything* transferred from the Royal Court. But the theatre was soon back to establishment works such as Dorothy Tutin impersonating Victoria in *Portrait Of A Queen* (1965), Sybil Thorndike, Athene Seyler, Richard Briers, Lewis Casson and Julia Lockwood in *Arsenic And Old Lace* (1966), and Leslie Phillips in *The Man Most Likely To . . .* (1968) which lasted for nearly two years.

In 1969, Peter Saunders bought the theatre from the Gatti family, put in air conditioning, showers in the dressing rooms, and repainted it. The pretty, mirrored entrance with a chandelier leads into the well-preserved auditorium where Moira Lister was seen in boudoir farces *Move Over, Mrs Markham* (1971) and *Key For Two* (1982); Glenda Jackson appeared in tragi-comedies *Stevie* (1977) and *Great And Small* (1983); Michael Frayn's *Benefactors* (1984) was premiered, and the prolific Alan Ayckbourn enjoyed another success with *Woman In Mind* (1987). In other words, the Vaudeville continues to supply top class West End shows in a pleasant setting.

Martin Jarvis and award-winning Julia McKenzie in Ayckbourn's Woman In Mind *(1986)*

THE VICTORIA PALACE

For decades, before air travel became the principal means of transport, most visitors from the Continent would not have had to go far in order to see a supreme example of English theatre architecture. Facing Victoria Station is an imposing and unusual white stone edifice, crowned with giant statues and a Baroque tower and dome. The classical facade, open loggia with Ionic columns high above the entrance, and festooned oval windows display the unmistakable touch of master theatre builder Frank Matcham, whose last remaining complete work in London this is.

Two buildings superseded the present Victoria Palace. Moy's Music Hall in the mid-19th century, renamed the Royal Standard Music Hall in 1863, was demolished in 1886 during the rebuilding of Victoria Station and environs. A new building on the site continued as a music hall until it, too, was pulled down in 1911. The Victoria Palace, built in the same year for impresario Alfred Butt, must have absorbed the music hall tradition of its antecedents into its very foundation stones for, with large music halls springing up all over the place, this was built to rival them all. The 1565-seat richly ornamented auditorium has a domed ceiling (the sliding roof keeps it cool in hot weather) and two tiers of three boxes on either side. Outside, on the pinnacle of the structure, was a gilded metal figure of Pavlova in full flight. It was said that the world's most famous ballerina superstitiously avoided looking at it every time she drove past by drawing the blinds of her car. The statue was taken down to protect it during the blitz, but its whereabouts today remain a mystery.

The Victoria Palace opened in November 1911 with a variety bill and continued in the same fashion, presenting variety and revues until 1934, except for the annual Christmas play *The Windmill Man* from 1920 to 1931. Among the revues were *The Show's The Thing* (1929)

'This lovely little theatre is one of the only remaining examples of a great and boisterous era.'

George Hoare

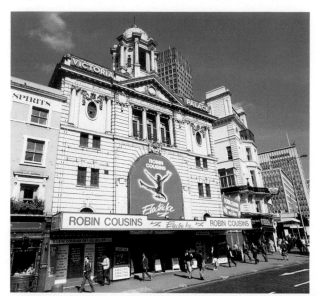

starring Gracie Fields, and *The Chelsea Follies* (1930) with Nervo and Knox, prior to their joining the Crazy Gang. In 1934 the notorious patriotic play, *Young England*, turned out to be one of the most curious hits in theatrical history. Walter Reynolds, the play's 83-year-old author, stated, 'I have aimed at providing three hours of clean wholesome entertainment, to put before you a bill of fare made up of the joys, the sorrows, the tears, the laughter, the soft romances, and the hard realities of our workaday existence.' But the melodramatic tale of a scoutmaster unjustly accused of theft from the scout funds was greeted with hilarity. Every platitude and sanctimonious situation was jeered, cheered and mocked by the crowds who flocked to see it.

Intentional humour was engendered when Seymour

Anton Rodgers (left) and Dennis Waterman in Windy City *(1982), a musical based on the famous Ben Hecht play,* The Front Page

Stephen Rea and Natasha Richardson in High Society *(1987), originally a film*

Hicks presented himself in a number of plays, including *The Miracle Man* (1935) in which his wife Ellaline Terriss made her farewell stage appearance at the age of 64. Revue returned in 1936 with *Let's Raise The Curtain* starring Florence Desmond and the incomparable Elisabeth Welch (still performing in her 80s, in the 1980s), and *Laughter Over London* with George Robey and Billy Bennett. In December 1937 the musical comedy *Me And My Girl*, with Lupino Lane as Bill Snibson doing the 'Lambeth Walk', started its 1046 performances until war broke out. Its huge popularity was initially created by a live broadcast of the show made from the theatre. It returned to the Victoria Palace in 1944 for another long run, and still proved its appeal at the Adelphi, and on Broadway, over 40 years later.

In 1947, the three comic duos – Flanagan and Allen, Naughton and Gold, and Nervo and Knox – who called themselves the Crazy Gang and had run riot at the Palladium in the 1930s, did the same for 15 years at the Victoria Palace. Joined by 'Monsewer' Eddie Gray, they appeared in *Together Again* (1947), *Knights Of Madness* (1950), *Ring Out The Bells* (1952), *Jokers Wild* (1954), *These Foolish Kings* (1956), *Clown Jewels* (1959) and *Young In Heart* (1960). The much-loved ancient comedians gave their final performance together on 19 May 1962.

For the next ten years the Victoria Palace was occupied by *The Black And White Minstrel Show*, a now racially discredited success from BBC Television. Variety remained the hallmark through the 1970s with singer-comedian Max Bygraves in two shows (1972 and 1974), and the crude 'Carry On' film team in *Carry On London* (1973), and other revues, until the arrival of the delightful Charles Strouse musical *Annie* (1978), which remained for three-and-a-half years. As at the Palladium, when variety faded, so musicals filled the bill. Cyd Charisse flashed her still lovely legs as Lady Hadwell in *Charlie Girl* (1986), a revival of the 1965 Adelphi hit, and Natasha Richardson, the daughter of Vanessa Redgrave, showed star quality in *High Society* (1987), adapted from the film with extra Cole Porter numbers. The big attraction of 1982 was when Elizabeth Taylor chose to make her London stage debut (farewell?) in Lillian Hellman's drama *The Little Foxes* at, of all places, the Victoria Palace!

THE WHITEHALL

In the broad avenue of administrative buildings that runs from Trafalgar Square, past the Cenotaph and Downing Street to the Houses of Parliament, stands an incongruous monument to the pursuit of pleasure. The Whitehall Theatre is a white hall or temple-like structure with tombstone-shaped windows. But the straight line of the unadorned facade masks a riotous assembly of Art Deco work within, executed by Marc-Henri and Laverdet. The black walls, an innovation in theatre decoration in England, the silver stripes on black over the proscenium arch, and the bold black octagonal shape on the ceiling form an ebony concerto in counterpoint to the sinuous patterns, and to the pastel colours of the murals and motif of musical instruments. Above the stage is a panel in which a nude Aphrodite seems to be trying to extricate herself from the tentacles of a sea-monster. The same tendril theme recurs in the centre of the ceiling and in the lights held in exotic flowers. With the Cubist-influenced murals,

the visitor gets a heavy whiff of the fashionable design of 1930, the year the theatre opened.

What it has had to offer in the way of entertainment over the years is of slightly less significance. The theatre's main claim to fame was as the home for 24 years of what became known as the Whitehall Farces, as distinct from the other Whitehall farces being played in the House of Commons down the road. In April 1961, Brian Rix, who managed the theatre and presented them, broke the Aldwych Theatre record of staging over 10 years of continuous productions of farce by one management in one theatre.

From its beginnings, comedy has been the main fare of the Whitehall. It was built by Edward A. Stone for the playwright Walter Hackett. He and his wife, Marion Lorne, managed the theatre for the first four years, she acting in the plays he wrote for her, their relationship

The striking auditorium and proscenium

illustrated by the title of the opening production – Hackett's *The Way To Treat A Woman* (a transfer from the Duke of York's.) Five further successful plays followed, one of them, *Good Losers* (1931), written by Hackett in collaboration with Michael Arlen. From 1934, a string of 'modern comedies' were produced, including St John Ervine's *Anthony And Anna* (1936) and a revival of George Bernard Shaw's *The Doctor's Dilemma* (1939).

During World War II, Alfred Esdaile presented *Whitehall Follies* (1942), a 'Non-Stop Revue' (continuous from 2 pm to 9 pm daily) featuring Phyllis Dixey, the West End's first stripper. Miss Dixey treated the art of ecdysism with expertise, carrying on a comic dialogue with the audience as she gracefully disrobed down to the last stitch. In fact, total nudity was permitted on stage in those days, provided the artiste did not

The octagonal ceiling design

'The Whitehall Theatre is so clean and simple in its line that it makes the new Government offices . . . of that great thoroughfare look as if they need a shave.'

Architect's Journal 1931

Brian Rix and Helen Jessop in One For The Pot, *one of the record-breaking Whitehall Farces which ran for over three years from 1961*

move her body. Phyllis Dixey would stand frozen (in both senses perhaps) in her naked glory while the audience cheered and applauded.

When Bernard Delfont took over the theatre in 1943, there was a brief return to clothed entertainment, but the public the Whitehall had built up for the revues did not take to Rodney Ackland's *The Dark River*, or John Steinbeck's *The Moon Is Down*, the latter about the German occupation of Norway. However, 'England's Queen of Glamour' was soon back in 'Non-Stop Revue Spectacles' like *Good Night Ladies!* So popular were they, that Miss Dixey took over the lease of the theatre herself in 1944. Interrupting her revealing shows was

A detail of the intricate wall decoration

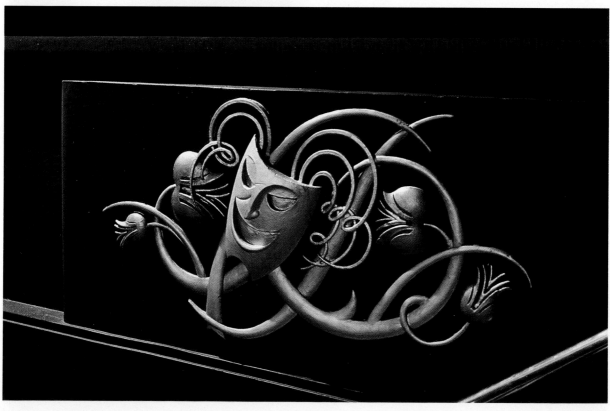

Priestley's When We Are Married *(1986) boasted a superb cast. Left to right (back): Timothy West, James Grout, Brian Murphy – front: Prunella Scales, Patricia Routledge, Elizabeth Spriggs*

R. F. Delderfield's R.A.F. farce *Worm's Eye View* (1945) with Ronald Shiner. After 500 performances it went on tour, returning in 1947 for another 1745 showings. A new era at the Whitehall had begun.

The farce that followed in 1950 was *Reluctant Heroes* by Colin Morris, starring Shiner again and Brian Rix, who was to play a gormless North Country goon forever losing his trousers in many more hits in the same genre. Far from his stage character, Rix was astute in the choice of plays he produced, the runs averaging three years each. They also reached the widest possible public by being regularly broadcast live on television. In the cast of *Reluctant Heroes* was John Chapman who wrote the next two successes, *Dry Rot* (1954) and *Simple Spyman* (1958). Another actor in the company, Ray Cooney, provided *One For The Pot* (1961) – written with Tony Hilton – and *Chase Me Comrade*(1964). Cooney explained how the latter, originally called *How's Your Father* about an escaped convict, came about: 'Brian and I agreed that it was just too old-fashioned – escaped convicts and jewels up the chimney at a time when Harold Pinter was establishing

himself! . . . As I was about to enter the Whitehall Theatre one of the most famous personalities of the day walked by – actually he glided by because it was Nureyev . . . Suddenly I knew how I could modernize *How's Your Father*. I'd change the whole plot of an escaped convict to a defecting Russian ballet dancer!'

The last of the Whitehall Farces was *Uproar In The House* (1967), which ran one-and-a-half years. In 1969, the theatre reverted to the Dixey days, when 'Revue Bar' impresario Paul Raymond took it over to present *Pyjama Tops*, a nudie show prominently featuring Fiona Richmond. After five profitable years, Raymond controversially turned the theatre into a museum of memorabilia of the two world wars. However, this breached the theatre's licensing conditions, and in 1985, Ian Albery's Maybox Group acquired it and began to present live shows again. Not all that different from the old Whitehall Farces, but with a political context, was John Wells' *Anyone For Denis?* (1982), in which Margaret Thatcher and her husband were impersonated. Unfortunately, the topical comedy was cut short by the advent of the Falklands war. But the tradition of comedy continued, albeit of a different style, with a glittering revival of Priestley's *When We Are Married* (1986), and Sharman MacDonald's *When I Was A Girl I Used To Scream And Shout* (1987), starring Julie Walters and Geraldine James.

WYNDHAM'S THEATRE

As the end of the 19th century drew to its close, a delightful new theatre opened its doors to a public who came to gaze on its delicate beauty. Today's audiences can still enjoy this jewel of a Victorian playhouse, named after one of England's finest actor-managers.

Charles Wyndham had long dreamed of building a theatre of his own, despite over 20 successful years of management at the Criterion. The Marquess of Salisbury, then Prime Minister, owned a site between Charing Cross Road and St Martin's Lane which Wyndham thought ideal. However, when he was unable to raise the required amount, Mary Moore, his leading lady (later his wife) asked a number of her friends in high places to stand as guarantors for a bank loan. The Australian-born W. G. R. Sprague was chosen as architect. He also built the New (now the Albery) for Wyndham on the other half of the same site a few years later and with a similar French classical facade. The French flavour of Wyndham's continues in the splen-

did Louis XVI decoration of the interior. Boucher was the inspiration for the pretty little ceiling in the foyer depicting angels and cherubs, and for the floral design on the circular ceiling above the pale blue and gold auditorium lit by a crystal chandelier. Above the picture frame proscenium are two male angels holding portraits of Oliver Goldsmith (left) and Richard Brinsley Sheridan (right), in front of a golden-winged bust of what is thought to be Mary Moore. An imposing bust of the theatre's eponymous owner greets one at the entrance, and the monograms C. W. and M. M. adorn each side of the stage.

The theatre opened on 16 November, 1899 in the presence of the Prince of Wales. Charles Wyndham and Mary Moore starred that night in the old Tom Robertson favourite, *David Garrick*. The next productions featured the tall and dashing Wyndham as Rostand's *Cyrano de Bergerac* (1900) and as a lawyer in Henry Arthur Jones' *Mrs Dane's Defence* of the same year.

> *'Sir Bronson Albery had been old for so long there were rumours . . . when the pipes in the theatre burst in midsummer . . . his cold feet were to blame.'*

Peter Ustinov

Actor-manager Charles Wyndham and his wife, the actress Mary Moore

With Frank Curzon managing on behalf of Wyndham, successes included Mabel Terry-Lewis (Ellen Terry's niece) in *Mrs Gorringe's Necklace*; J. M. Barrie's *Little Mary* (both 1903); *When Knights Were Bold* (1907); and *An Englishman's Home* (1909), written anonymously by 'A Patriot'. In fact, the play, about an invasion of England, was by Gerald du Maurier's soldier brother, Guy, who would be killed in World War I. It caused a flurry of patriotism and increased recruitment into the Territorial Army. When Gerald joined Curzon as manager, he revived his *Raffles* (1914), created the role of the drunken painter in Barrie's *Dear Brutus* (1917), played 'Sapper's' hero *Bulldog Drummond* (1921) with infinite charm, and appeared opposite the outrageous American star Tallulah Bankhead, making her London debut, in *The Dancers* (1923).

From 1926, the theatre was given over to the crime dramas of Edgar Wallace until the author's death in Hollywood in 1932. Wallace took an apartment above the theatre, which is now used as an office and still contains the large armchair built to support his portly frame. Audiences chilled to *The Ringer* (1926), *The Calendar* (1929), *On The Spot* (1930), *The Old Man* (1931), *The Case Of The Frightened Lady* (1931) and

The Green Pack (1932). For *Smoky Cell* (1930), Wallace had the macabre idea of making the public believe they were witnesses to an execution by electric chair in America, even to the issuing of reproduction journalists' cards instead of ordinary theatre tickets.

The Wallace collection gave way to a patchwork of productions under the management of stepbrothers Howard Wyndham and Bronson Albery up to the outbreak of war. In 1934, they presented the imperial drama *Clive Of India*; *The Maitlands*, the second and last play by Ronald MacKenzie, in which John Gielgud played a seedy schoolmaster; and Joyce Carey in her own play *Sweet Aloes*. The Broadway comedy *Three Men On A Horse* (1936), Gerald Savory's *George And Margaret* (1937), and Esther McCracken's *Quiet Wedding* (1938) blithely followed.

The war years were enlivened by the 1059 performances of *Quiet Weekend* (1940), the sequel to *Quiet Wedding*, and a 'blitz time afternoon all-star

Sir Alec Guinness, here with Eileen Atkins, starred in his own distinguished production of T.S. Eliot's The Cocktail Party *in 1968*

The Wyndham's stage has been graced over the last two decades by a bevy of fine actresses – Dulcie Gray (*Candida*, 1960); Celia Johnson (*Chin Chin*, 1960; *The Dame Of Sark*, 1974); Vanessa Redgrave (*The Prime Of Miss Jean Brodie*, 1966; *Ghosts*, 1986); Diana Rigg (*Abelard And Heloise*, 1970), and Faye Dunaway (*Circe And Bravo*, 1986). The religious rock musical *Godspell* (1972) was here for four years, during which time up-and-coming stars David Essex, Marti Webb and Jeremy Irons had roles. On the door of the star dressing room are scrawled the names of stage luminaries past and present. The history of the Wyndham's suggests there will be many more in the future.

Colin Blakely and Rosemary Harris shone in Arthur Miller's powerful drama, All My Sons *(1981)*

entertainment' called *Diversion* (1939), featuring Edith Evans, Bernard Miles, Dorothy Dickson, and two young men who shared a dressing room – Peter Ustinov and Derek Bogerde (Dirk Bogarde). Ustinov's play, *The Banbury Nose* (1944), came in for a few months before *Years Between* (1945) by Daphne du Maurier who, as a child, had watched her father perform from the wings of Wyndham's.

Both Edith Evans (now a Dame) and Peter Ustinov returned to Wyndham's after the war, she in James Bridie's *Daphne Laureola* (1947), and he in *The Love Of Four Colonels* (1951), his first popular success as a playwright. However, for most of the 1950s, the theatre was occupied by Sandy Wilson's tuneful 20s musical pastiche called *The Boy Friend* (1954). The show, which began modestly at the small Players' Theatre, ran a record 2078 performances, and launched Julie Andrews on Broadway. After the flappers left, a flap was caused by Joan Littlewood's controversial Theatre Workshop productions of 20-year-old Shelagh Delaney's *A Taste Of Honey* and Brendan Behan's *The Hostage* (both 1959), bringing Wyndham's sharply back into the contemporary world. The same company would return in 1963 with *Oh What A Lovely War!*, a bitter attack, through song and satire, on the Great War, later filmed by Richard Attenborough.

WYNDHAMS

ARTHUR MILLER'S
ALL MY SONS

AGNIFICENT
NEW PRODUCTION"

WYNDHAM'S
THEATRE

ALL MY
SONS

"SPLENDID PLAY"

ALL MY SONS

"FINE PRODU

OTHER THEATRES OF INTEREST

Apart from the forty-four principal theatres illustrated in this book, there are innumerable others that add to the richness of London's theatrical life. These include dozens of 'fringe', pub, community, club, special interest and suburban theatres. I have had to make an invidious choice of those I consider the most consistently lively and important at the time of writing and, inevitably, there are regrettable exclusions – particularly as the growth rate of these venues is prodigious.

THE ALMEIDA

The Almeida Theatre Company was conceived by Lebanese-born, Oxford-educated Pierre Audi in 1979, when he acquired a derelict Salvation Army Hall in an unfashionable part of Islington in North London. In a few years, with the essential aid of the now-defunct Greater London Council, Audi established a fashionable theatrical centre for adventurous audiences. Here, they have been stimulated by innovative drama, modern dance and an annual festival of contemporary music, all of which include a strong foreign representation. In 1985, the Almeida staged an acclaimed production of Dostoyevsky's *The Possessed*, directed by the celebrated Russian, Yuri Lyubimov. Now, funded principally by the Greater London Arts Council, it has completed its third phase of a building programme in which a circle has been added, making up a 300-seat capacity, and new dressing rooms.

THE ARTS

Sandwiched between doorways of shops and restaurants in tiny Great Newport Street – in the heart of Chinese Soho – is the Arts Theatre. At its height, during the 1940s and 1950s, the Arts Theatre Club was called by a critic 'a pocket National Theatre'. Certainly, the importance of this 339-seat venue over the years cannot be underestimated – especially during the period when censorship still held sway over English theatre. The Arts was set up in 1927 to stage unlicensed and experimental plays under club conditions, thus eluding the heavy hand of the Lord Chamberlain. One of the first productions was of the banned John Van Druten

drama *Young Woodley* (1927). During the period between 1942 and 1952 when actor Alec Clunes ran the theatre with much success, many plays had their premieres here, including Christopher Fry's *The Lady's Not For Burning* (1948), which first brought the author into the limelight. Peter Hall, then aged only 25, was the director of the Arts from 1955 to 1956, his most famous production being the British premiere of Samuel Beckett's *Waiting For Godot* (1955). Harold Pinter's first success, *The Caretaker* (1960) was unveiled here and, in 1962, the Royal Shakespeare Company presented six new plays and two revivals. In 1966, Caryl Jenner's Unicorn Theatre for Children took over the building and, aside from intermittent adult plays (two hits were *Kennedy's Children*, 1975, and Tom Stoppard's double bill, *Dirty Linen* and *New Found Land*, 1976), films and late-night entertainments, children are its main audience today.

THE BUSH

The Bush sprouted in 1972, becoming one of the first in a forest of pub theatres that sprang up in London in the early 1970s, and has been in the forefront of fringe theatre ever since. Its high reputation was gained by an astute choice of new plays by unknown writers, many of whose works went on to fill larger, West End theatres. Doug Lucie's *Progress* and Sharman McDonald's *When I Was A Girl I Used To Scream And Shout* are just two examples. Crowds flock to this upstairs room of the Old Bush pub off Shepherd's Bush Green, the stimulating entertainment they find there compensating for the fact that the three-sided, 100-seat auditorium is one of the most uncomfortable in London. The atmosphere, however, is vibrant and warm, and one can enjoy a drink during the performance.

In June 1987, the Bush suffered a fire which caused considerable damage, thus necessitating their productions to be presented in other venues for some months while repairs were carried out. Ironically, it was the second prominent fringe venue within a matter of weeks – the Tricycle in Kilburn was the first – to meet such a fate.

THE DONMAR WAREHOUSE

Originally known just as The Warehouse, the Donmar, in the heart of Covent Garden, is one of the most enterprising and enjoyable of fringe theatres in London, offering genuine 'alternative' theatre without solemnity. It is also a venue where a mixed crowd (age, sex, class and race) can enjoy a show after 10 p.m. on Fridays, Saturdays and Sundays, and drink until 1.30 a.m. The two-level square room with seating around three sides of the acting area, was used as a rehearsal room from 1961 until 1976. Then, from 1977-1981, the Royal Shakespeare Company used it very effectively as a studio theatre until they moved to the Barbican. Among their noted productions here were the stark Ian McKellen-Judi Dench *Macbeth*, *Piaf* and *Educating Rita*. In 1981 Ian Albery formed a non-profit making company called Omega to take it over. The name of the theatre derives from that of Ian Albery's father Donald (Don) and his friend, the dancer Margot Fonteyn (Mar); and from the fact that the building had been a banana warehouse in the 19th century. It is the only theatre of its size (244 seats) that relies wholly on the box-office for its revenue. Thanks to the energetic administrative team led by Nica Burns, it pays its way with a diverse programme of entertainments, ranging from experimental Shakespeare to cabaret with performers such as Barbara Cook.

GREENWICH

Not far from the *Cutty Sark*, moored at Greenwich Pier, and the National Maritime Museum, is the attractive and spacious Greenwich Theatre, built in 1969 in the shell of a late 19th-century music hall. Initially under the direction of actor Ewan Hooper, the one-tier, raked 426-seat auditorium has housed presentations of a wide selection of new plays, musicals and revivals. Works by John Mortimer (*A Voyage Round My Father*, 1970), Peter Nichols (*Forget-Me-Not-Lane*, 1971), Alan Ayckbourn (*The Norman Conquests*, 1974) and Julian Mitchell (*Another Country*, 1981) were first seen here, as well as regular productions of Ibsen, Chekhov, O'Neill and Tennessee Williams. The theatre has also attracted leading performers and directors up the river.

There is a restaurant, coffee bar, and exhibition area, and one can also enjoy a drink at the Rose and Crown next door, which dates from 1888.

THE HALF MOON

The Half Moon is the living proof that there is a vibrant theatrical life outside the West End. It was born in 1972 in a disused synagogue in Aldgate in the East End, then moved seven years later to a converted Methodist Chapel in the Mile End Road. It has become a vastly popular centre, not only with 'slummers' from up West, but with the local people, because the majority of plays presented here are meaningful to this working-class district. One of their biggest hits was *Trafford Tanzi* (1980), a 'battle of the sexes' wrestling comedy by Claire Luckham, wife of the present artistic director, Chris Bond. A splendid small-scale production of Stephen Sondheim's musical *Sweeney Todd*, based on Bond's play of the same name, opened the new 400-seat theatre in 1983, built on the same site with private contributions, local and Arts Council money. The Chapel remains as a comfortable bar and restaurant with a small gallery for exhibitions. This characterful venue also boasts a production manager called Spiderman.

THE HAMPSTEAD THEATRE CLUB

Just as the Half Moon makes its appeal to East Enders, so much of the fare on offer at the Hampstead Theatre Club (there is a token annual membership fee) seems to be aimed at the well-heeled liberal Hampsteaders, many of the plays making an easy transfer to the West End. However, much adventurous new work has been done, and the present Artistic Director, Michael Attenborough, son of Sir Richard, is particularly determined to encourage new writing. Contemporary American playwrights such as Sam Shepard (*Buried Child*, 1980), Lyle Kessler (*Orphans*, 1986), and Donald Freed (*Circe And Bravo*, 1986) have been well represented. The Club was founded by James Roose-Evans in 1959 in a small hall next door to the Everyman Cinema, itself one of the first little theatres in the 1920s. The Camden Council built the new theatre in 1962 opposite the Swiss Cottage pub on the busy Finchley Road, the street on which American director Alan Schneider was killed while crossing to the theatre. Although built over 25 years ago, and despite some enlargement, the small building with its one-tier raked 174-seat auditorium, still gives the impression of being a temporary structure. The foyer and bar are far too cramped to hold even half the capacity audience. But it is an important and extremely active theatrical force in North London, whose residents contributed to the premises with subscriptions that bought seats which bear little brass plaques engraved with the giver's name.

THE ICA
(The Institute of Contemporary Arts)

It is a far cry from the basement of the recently defunct Academy Cinema in Oxford Street, where the ICA started in 1947 as a gallery and a meeting place for artists, to the spacious, modern premises inside the splendid John Nash terrace building on the Mall, opposite St James's Park, that is now its home. When they took it over in 1968, the founders declared, 'The Ivory Tower has been demolished. The ICA has become an open forum and an organization that jealously guards its independence.' The expanding institute contains three galleries, two cinemas, a video library, a seminar room, a bookshop, a bar, a cafe and a 200-seat theatre. The latter mounts a wide range of international new plays, operas, music and dance, reflecting and promoting every new – and sometimes provocative – development in the performing arts over recent years.

THE KINGS HEAD

One of the very first pub theatres in London was started in the large back room of the Kings Head Pub in Islington by American producer Dan Crawford in 1971. The 120-seat space has provided scope for a wide variety of shows of quality over the years with several transfers to the West End and Broadway. Rather less committed to radical plays than many other fringe theatres, with a penchant for small-scale musicals such as *Mr Cinders* (1983), it tries to retain a policy of six-week runs. The

Kings Head is one of the rare pub theatres where audiences can partake of a decent, inexpensive meal at tables in the auditorium before the show, as well as being able to drink during it.

THE MAYFAIR

This comfortable, modern 310-seat theatre is situated inside the swanky Mayfair Hotel, just off Berkeley Square. It was built in 1963 by American impresario brothers, Edward J. and Harry Lee Danziger, who transformed the old Candlelight Room, where big bands broadcast in the 1930s, into an adaptable raked auditorium. The opening production, which starred Ralph Richardson as the Father in Pirandello's *Six Characters In Search Of An Author*, was given on a bare stage with exposed wings, no proscenium, and a great deal of trick lighting. Also on a bare stage was the four-man revue *Beyond The Fringe* (1964), transferred from the Fortune, which ran well over two years. It has enjoyed mixed fortunes over the years, until Richard Todd in *The Business Of Murder* (1980) settled in for a continuing seven years. The hotel's guests are protected by sound-proofing from any nasty goings-on in the theatre.

THE OPEN AIR THEATRE, REGENT'S PARK

Despite the vagaries of the English weather, annual summer seasons of Shakespeare have been given in the open air since the turn of the century in Regent's Park (then called the Royal Botanical Gardens). A permanent *al fresco* theatre was constructed in 1933, and old-time Shakespearean actor Robert Atkins ran it from 1939 to 1961. Whether chilly, scorching, rainy (a marquee is erected) or windy, audiences still enjoy the unique experience (jet planes notwithstanding) of watching the pastoral comedies of Shakespeare, or plays by Shaw, Jonson etc in a timeless green glade. Blankets and hot drinks are available, if necessary.

THE PLAYERS THEATRE

Victorian Music Hall is being kept alive in an unlikely place, tucked under Hungerford Bridge near Charing Cross Railway Station. The Players Theatre Club, called variously the Arches, the Hungerford, Gatti's, and Charing Cross Music Hall since 1863, has its entrance in a railway arch. When Music Hall faded away, the building was used as a cinema, a boxing venue, and an Auxiliary Fire Service Depot during World War II. It was in 1945 that Leonard Sachs and Jean Anderson acquired the 300-seat theatre underneath the arches, refurbished it, and recaptured the spirit of the 'lost Empires'. Old-time Victorian Music Hall and an annual Victorian pantomime, contrasting with the diluted, commercial versions elsewhere, are its regular fare. In 1953, Sandy Wilson's 20s pastiche musical, *The Boy Friend*, had its premiere here before moving on to the West End, Broadway and the Movies. The Players – 'Late Joy' Company continue to provide an unusual night out and an authentic trip into London's theatrical past.

THE PLAYHOUSE

It is heartening that in an era when theatres are more likely to be closed than opened, the Playhouse should be reversing the trend. After 36 years otherwise engaged, it has taken its attractive place again among the leading London theatres. In fact, John Earl, writing in *Curtains* in 1981 said, 'This outstanding theatre should be restored to public use as quickly as possible, with minimum disturbance to its architectural character'. The Royal Avenue, as it was called until 1907, was opened in March 1882 in an unusual location: a part of Northumberland Avenue off Trafalgar Square, under which runs a section of the Charing Cross Railway station. Although its Portland stone exterior dates from then, its interior has been remodelled twice – the second time in 1905 after the theatre had been wrecked by the collapse of part of the station above.

Many great names and productions have been associated with the Playhouse. George Alexander (later of the now extinct St James' Theatre) started his career here as actor-manager, his successors being Cyril Maude, Frank Curzon and Gladys Cooper. The regal Miss Cooper ran it from 1917 to 1933, and starred in many of the plays. The theatre also saw the premiere of Shaw's *Arms And The Man*, and the long run of Charles Hawtrey in a *A Message From Mars*. In 1951, however, it became a BBC studio for broadcasts of radio shows with a live audience. After lying idle for some years, the Playhouse reopened as a theatre in September, 1987, under the artistic directorship of David Porter, with a musical called *Girlfriends*. Now, once again, playgoers can appreciate its fine plasterwork, curved walls, balustraded balconies and dome. Whether it has a future as prestigious as its past remains to be seen.

THE RIVERSIDE STUDIOS

At the turn of the century, on the site of the present arts centre near Hammersmith Bridge, stood a foundry and workers' cottages. Then, in 1933, a film studio was built with two sound stages, now the two studio theatres, where pictures starring James Mason, Ann Todd and Michael Redgrave among others were made. In 1954, the BBC bought the studio and used it for recording many of their most popular TV programmes including *Hancock's Half-Hour* and *Dixon Of Dock Green*. A further change took place in 1974 when Hammersmith Council transformed the Riverside Studios into an arts complex containing an adventurous art gallery, an excellent bookshop, a bar, a canteen and two theatres. In late 1987, a new 200-seat cinema opened in the old Dubbing Theatre. Over the years (ten of them under the artistic direction of Peter Gill), the Riverside has established a reputation both as a community centre and as a forum for a diversity of progressive entertainment, with a strong accent on post-modernist dance and plays. It has also regularly hosted famous foreign ensembles such as Dario Fo's company from Italy and Tadeus Kantor's Polish troupe, as well as showcasing major fringe successes from The Edinburgh Festival.

THE ROYALTY

The Royalty, enclosed in an office block, was the first new theatre to be built in London in a 29-year period. It was constructed in 1960 on the site of the old Stoll Theatre in Kingsway that was demolished in 1957. The Stoll had opened in 1911 as the London Opera House, conceived by American impresario Oscar Hammerstein as a rival to the Royal Opera, Covent Garden. But it lost the contest, and was soon presenting revues, musical comedies and pantomimes instead. It became the Stoll Picture Theatre in 1917, only returning to the fold in 1942 as the Stoll Theatre where ballet, opera, musicals and ice spectaculars were staged. After *Kismet* (1955) ran for 648 performances, Laurence Olivier and Vivien Leigh appeared in their successful Stratford-Upon-Avon production of *Titus Andronicus* (1957), the last show to be performed at the Stoll. The Royalty opened with Alfred Lunt and Lynn Fontanne in Friedrich Durrenmatt's *The Visit* (1960), but the building quickly became a cinema. Reclaimed again for the performing arts, it presented *Oh Calcutta* (1970), which ran for over three years. It then was lost again as a theatre when Thames Television used it as a studio until the revival of Andrew Lloyd Webber and Tim Rice's first hit, *Joseph And The Amazing Technicolor Dreamcoat* (1986). The 922-seat auditorium is also used as a concert hall and a conference centre.

THE SHAW

The Shaw Theatre, named after the great Irish playwright, is situated in the borough where George Bernard Shaw was a Socialist member of the council. Camden Council built the 458-seat, one-tier theatre in 1971 as part of a new library building, finally providing a home for the famous National Youth Theatre Company. The company's founder, former actor and schoolteacher Michael Croft (he died in 1986), presented Shakespeare and modern plays, most of them written by Peter Terson, for large casts of performers under 18. Alternating with the youth theatre at the Shaw, was the Dolphin Theatre Company, a professional troupe specializing in the classics. Vanessa Redgrave as Viola in *Twelfth Night* (1971), Mia Farrow in Barrie's *Mary Rose* (1972) and Susan Hampshire in *The Taming Of The Shrew* (1974) all appeared here. After severe financial troubles in the early 80s resulting from the loss of their grant, the National Youth Theatre was given a great boost in 1987 when a private firm came to their rescue and Prince Edward became their patron. Aside from the NYT summer season, the theatre is devoted to a mixed programme of events aimed at members of the local community, and some interesting plays.

STRATFORD EAST THEATRE ROYAL

Although Joan Littlewood's Theatre Workshop was resident here only from 1953 to 1964, it was a landmark in the long history of the Theatre Royal built in 1884 in the East End of London, in Chaucer's Stratford-atte-Bowe. For most of its life the theatre was the home of 'blood and thunder' melodramas, twice-nightly variety and revues at cheap prices. It was derelict when Littlewood's touring company took it over, and established 'a British People's Theatre'. The company was originally founded by a group of artists who were 'dissatisfied with the commercial theatre on artistic, social and political grounds.' Among their greatest successes were *A Taste Of Honey, The Hostage* (both 1958), *Fings Aint Wot They Used To Be* (1959), *Sparrers Can't Sing* (1960), and *Oh What A Lovely War!* (1963). In 1973, Stephen Sondheim paid a visit to Stratford East to see Chris Bond's version of the melodrama *Sweeney Todd*. So impressed was he by its 'combination of charm and creepiness' that he turned it into the well-known musical. Thanks to the Government Listing of buildings, the Theatre Royal, graded II, was saved from demolition in the early 70s when massive clearances took place in Stratford town centre. It now stands, a relic of the Victorian age on the edge of a modern shopping precinct, still attracting audiences into its warm East End atmosphere – but there is nothing old-fashioned about the programme of new plays, mounted under the artistic directorship of Philip Hedley.

THE TRICYCLE

In May 1987, one of London's most enterprising Fringe theatres was gutted by fire, ironically during the run of a play called *Burning Point*. This disaster ended – temporarily – the run of highly individual productions mounted since it was founded in 1980 with the help of the Brent Borough Council. Under the artistic directorship of Nicolas Kent, The Tricycle developed a policy which included the encouragement of Irish and black writers, in an area where many Irish and black people live. In fact, one of their last pre-Inferno productions was James Baldwin's *The Amen Corner* (1987) which transferred to the West End. The Tricycle also included, in its limited space, a restaurant and bar, gallery and book stall. A rebuilding appeal for £50,000 was launched so that the building would once again fill a much-needed gap in the area of Kilburn, otherwise not renowned for cultural venues.

THE WESTMINSTER

The Westminster Theatre, conveniently situated close to Buckingham Palace, was originally a chapel that was converted into the St James Picture Theatre in 1924. In 1931, an ex-pupil of the nearby Westminster School transformed it into a 603-seat theatre, with the former crypt becoming the dressing rooms. The owner was A.B. Horne, who called himself Anmer Hall after his Norfolk ancestral home. The new theatre established a good reputation in the 1930s and 1940s, presenting plays by Ibsen, Shaw, Granville Barker, O'Neill, Eliot and Pirandello. J. B. Priestley and Robert Donat were involved in its management at different times, the latter appearing in a successful revival of Oscar Wilde's *An Ideal Husband* (1943). The hit of the 1950s was *Dial M For Murder* (1952), which ran 425 performances. In 1960, however, the Moral Rearmament Movement took control, and used the building for their own propaganda purposes. Commercial plays do return spasmodically, but the Westminster remains generally outside the mainstream. It is also the only London theatre where no alcohol is served.

THE YOUNG VIC

In 1946, a company called the Young Vic was formed to play to children at the Old Vic under the directorship of George Devine, who later became head of the English Stage Company at the Royal Court. Due to financial problems, the company was disbanded in 1951. The present Young Vic, in an unattractive building a few hundred yards from the Old Vic, was the brain child of Frank Dunlop, then a director at the National Theatre. The large square space enclosed by tiered wooden benches holding 456 people, and a studio of 150 seats, was set up to play ancient and modern classics to the under-25s, with Shakespeare predominating. Today, its general quality, and interesting and unusual productions such as the revival of Ibsen's *Ghosts* (1986), starring Vanessa Redgrave, attracts an audience that includes many of more mature years.

INDEX

Phyllis Nielsen
Neilson-Terry, Dennis 158
Nerina, Nadia 149
Nervo, Jimmy 120, 122, 174, 175
Nestroy, Johann 106
Neville, John 114
New Adelphi Theatre *see* Adelphi
Theatre
Newley, Anthony 135, 139
New London Theatre 107-109
New Moon, The 60
New Opera Company 153
New Princes Theatre *see*
Shaftesbury Theatre
New Theatre *see* Albery Theatre
New Victoria Cinema *see* Apollo
Victoria Theatre
New Victoria Palace *see* Old Vic
Theatre
New Watergate Club, The 46
Next Time I'll Sing To You 53
Nicholas Nickleby 11, 21
Nichols, Peter 48
Night And Day 126
Night In Venice, A 37
Nilsson, Birgit 148
Nippy 131
Night Must Fall 64
Night Of The Garter 166
Night Out, A 107
Noah 16
Noises Off 98, 160
No Medals 172
Nono 20
No, No, Nanette 117
Norma 87, 148
Normal Heart, The 17
Norman, Frank 76
Norman Conquests, The 80
No Room At The Inn 108
Northcote, John 62
Norton, Frederick 88
No Sex Please We're British 65,
76, 168
No Time For Sergeants 90
Notorious Mrs Ebbsmith, The 73
Novello, Ivor 12, 24, 26, 60, 62,
75, 88, 92, 115, 118, 120, 132
Nude With Violin 80
Nunn, Trevor 33, 36, 108, 118,
132
Nureyev, Rudolph 149
Nutcracker, The 149, 152

Oberon 146
Obey, André 16
O'Casey, Sean 26, 70
Octoroon, The 12
Odds And Ends 23
Oh Calcutta! 63, 65
Oh What A Lovely War! 182
Okay For Sound 122
O'Keeffe, John 50, 162
Oklahoma 57, 60, 71
Old Acquaintance 28
Old Bachelor, The 96
Old Country, The 139

Oldman, Gary 94
Old Man, The 181
Old Times 85
Old Vic Theatre 16, 17, 33, 102,
104, 110-114, 151
Old Lady Shows Her Medals, The
16
Oliver 17
Oliver, Stephen 114
Oliver Twist 11, 17, 87, 165
Olivier, Sir Laurence 16, 17, 39,
56, 76, 92, 102, 104, 112, 114,
115, 118, 123, 126, 142, 143,
158
Olivier Theatre *see* National
Theatre
O'Malley, Mary 142
On Approval 70
Once A Catholic 142
O'Neill, Eugene 17, 24, 106, 166
One For The Pot 179
One Over The Eight 68
Once In A Lifetime 138
On The Razzle 106
On The Spot 181
On Your Toes 117, 118
Oresteia, The 106
Orfeo ed Euridice 148
Orphans 28
Orton, Joe 94, 139
Osborne, John 39, 118, 140, 142
Othello 10, 92, 114
Other Places 65
Otherwise Engaged 139
O'Toole, Peter 39, 114, 164
Otway, Thomas 98
Our American Cousin 84
Our Betters 78
Our Boys 169
Our Girls 169
Outward Bound 75
Over The Moon 132

Pacific 60
Pacino, Al 66, 69
Paddy The Next Best Thing 158
Page, Austin 75
Page, Elaine 132
Page, Geraldine 156
Page, Gertrude 158
Paint Your Wagon 90
Pair of Spectacles, A 73
Palace Of Truth, The 133
Palace Theatre 36, 115-118, 119
Palace Theatre of Varieties
see Palace Theatre
Pal Joey 162
Palladium Minstrels, The 120
Palladium Theatre 119, 122, 175
Palmer, Lilli 139
Papp, Joseph 76
Park, Merle 149
Parker, Cecil 128
Parnell, Val 122
Party, The 114
Passing Show, The 116
Passing Show of 1915, The 116

Patent Theatres 10, 141
Patience 157
Patriot For Me, A 142
Patti, Adelina 147
Pavlova, Anna 115
Payn, Graham 128
Peach, C. Stanley 82
Pears, Peter 152
Perdition 143
Peer Gynt 17
Peg O' My Heart 46
Peg Woffington 135
Pélissier, Harry Gabriel 26
Pelléas et Mélisande 133, 148
Pell Mell 24
Penelope 46
Penny Plain 156
People's National Theatre, The
64, 70
Percival, Michael 108
Percy, Edward 156
Percy, Esme 80
Peter Grimes 152
Peter Pan 12, 16, 66, 68, 107, 122
Petrified Forest, The 80
Pettingell, Frank 155, 166
Phantom Of The Opera, The 87,
90
Phantom Of The Opera, The
(film) 54
Phelps, Samuel 84, 151
Philanthropist, The 142
Phillips, Leslie 172
Phillpots, Eden 143
Phipps, C.J. 73, 86, 91, 133, 157,
169
Phoenix Theatre 37, 123-126,
130
Piccadilly Hayride 135
Piccadilly Theatre 14, 64, 127-
129
Pick-Up Girl 132
Pickwick Papers, The 11
Pieces Of Eight 28
Pilbeam, Nova 122
Pilot, The 10
Pineapple Poll 149
Pinero, Sir Arthur Wing 12, 16,
73, 75, 76, 142
Pink Dominoes 49
Pinney-Reed, Beatrice May 87
Pinter, Harold 21, 53, 63, 64, 65,
85, 98, 106, 179
Plaintiff In A Pretty Hat 156
Planché, James Robinson 146
Playfair, Sir Nigel 19, 96
Pleasence, Donald 65, 68
Pleasure Of His Company, The
126
Plough And The Stars, The 70
Plowright, Joan (Lady Olivier)
66, 80, 94, 114, 129
Plunder 20
Poel, William 112
Polunin, Vladimir 125
Pomeroy, Jan 37
Poor Bitos 68

Porter, Cole 117, 175
Portman, Eric 126, 156, 162
Portrait Of A Queen 172
Potash And Perlmutter 138
*Potash And Perlmutter In
Society* 138
Potiphar's Wife 78
Potter, John 81
Potting Shed, The 80
Power, Tyrone 108
Power And The Glory, The 126
Power Without Glory 71
Pravda 106
Premise, The 46
Price, Dennis 138
Price, Nancy 64, 70
Priestley, J.B. 53, 63, 64, 80, 88,
92, 106, 155, 168, 179
Prime Of Miss Jean Brodie, The
182
Primrose 107
Prince And The Showgirl, The
126
Prince Edward Theatre 30, 37,
130-132
Prince of Wales Theatre 91, 133-
135
Princess, The 168
Princess Charming 117
Princess Ida 157
Prince's Theatre *see* Prince of
Wales Theatre
Princes Theatre *see* Shaftesbury
Theatre
Prinsep, Anthony 78
Printemps, Yvonne 20, 92
Prisoner, The 80
*Private Ear And The Public Eye,
The* 80
Private Lives 28, 68, 123, 139
Private Secretary, The 133
Profligate, The 73
Prokofiev, Serge 44
Promise, The 72
Promises Promises 135
Prowse, Juliet 126, 135
Puccini, Giacomo 66, 147
Purcell, Henry 99
Pygmalion 87, 164
Pyjama Game, The 44
Pyjama Tops 76, 179

Quadrille 124
Quaker Girl, The 10
Quality Street 170
Quartermaine, Leon 92
Quayle, Anthony 156
Queen Elizabeth Hall 102
Queensbury All-Services Club
132
Queen's Theatre 77, 136-139
Queen's Theatre (destroyed
1705) *see* Her Majesty's Theatre
Queen Was In The Parlour, The
155
Quiet Wedding 181
Quiet Weekend 181

PICTURE CREDITS

AMBASSADOR'S THEATRE: 23

CATHERINE ASHMORE (Dominic Photography): 40, 44

CLIVE BARDA: 144

BBC HULTON PICTURE LIBRARY: 8, 75, 123, 178 (above)

PETER BLOOMFIELD: 33

BRITISH TRAVEL ASSOCIATION (Britain On View):
19 (above), 43, 98 (above), 117 (above), 130, 141, 157, 161, 167, 183

NOBBY CLARK (Courtesy of Sue Hyman Associates):
30 (below)

DEE CONWAY: 24 (below), 55 (below), 72 (below), 126, 139 (below), 148, 152, 153

DONALD COOPER: 13, 17, 20, 28 (above), 36, 48 (below), 52 (above), 56, 65 (below), 76, 80, 85 (below), 90, 101 (below), 107, 117 (below), 118, 120 (below), 122, 129 (below), 160 (above), 164, 168 (above), 172, 174 (below), 175, 179

ZOE DOMINIC: 16 (below), 28 (below), 31 (above), 38 48 (above), 60, 62 (above), 65 (above), 69 (above), 94 (above), 108 (below), 113 (above), 129 (above), 132, 139 (above), 149, 182

E.T. ARCHIVES: 58, 146, 158, 170 (below)

JOHN HAYNES: 6 (below)

TOM HUSTLER: 134 (inset), 135 (above)

NEIL LIBBERT: 7

SUSAN LOPPERT: 14, 22, 46, 73, 81, 83, 154

LYRIC HAMMERSMITH ARCHIVE: 96, 97

ANGUS McBEAN (Courtesy of Mander & Mitchenson) 9, 78 (below)

DOUG McKENZIE (Professional Photographic Services)
11, 30 (above), 49, 63, 71, 79, 89, 93, 125 (above), 128, 171, 177 (above)

DOUG McKENZIE (Courtesy of Stoll Theatres) 25, 57, 61, 62 (below), 121, 138, 147 (above)

KIRSTY McLAREN: Contents and title page, 10, 15, 18, 19 (below), 26, 27, 29, 31 (below), 37, 39, 41, 45, 47, 50, 51, 53, 54, 55 (above), 64, 69 (below), 74, 77, 86, 88, 91, 99, 101 (above), 108 (above), 109, 111, 113 (below), 115, 116, 119, 120 (above), 124, 125 (below), 127, 131, 133, 134 (exterior), 135 (below), 136, 137, 143, 145, 150, 151, 159, 160 (below), 162, 163, 165, 168 (below), 169, 173, 176, 177 (below), 178 (below), 180, 181 (below)

THE RAYMOND MANDER AND JOE MITCHENSON COLLECTION: 66, 68, 70, 78 (above), 82, 92, 95, 112, 156 (above), 181 (above)

MARY EVANS PICTURE LIBRARY: Half-title, 12, 59, 84, 87, 166, 170 (above)

NATIONAL THEATRE ARCHIVE: 6 (above), 102, 103, 106

BERTRAM PARK: 16

PETER SAUNDERS MANAGEMENT: 24 (above), 155

THEATRE MUSEUM (Photo by Houston Rogers) 140

CLIVE TOTMAN: 32, 34, 35

TOWN HOUSE PUBLICITY: 110

ALEX VON KOETTLITZ: 21 (below), 42, 52 (below), 72 (above), 85 (above), 94 (below), 98 (below), 100, 104, 105, 114, 142, 147

REG WILSON: 156 (below)